The July 2013 Senior Loan Officer Opinion Survey on Bank Lending Practices

The July 2013 Senior Loan Officer Opinion Survey on Bank Lending Practices addressed changes in the standards and terms on, and demand for, bank loans to businesses and households over the past three months. The survey also contained special questions about changes in banks' lending standards on, and demand for, the three main types of commercial real estate (CRE) loans over the past year, and on the current levels of banks' lending standards for many types of business and household loans relative to longer-term norms. In the July survey, domestic banks, on balance, reported having eased their lending standards and having experienced stronger demand in most loan categories over the past three months. This summary is based on the responses from 73 domestic banks and 22 U.S. branches and agencies of foreign banks.[1]

Regarding loans to businesses, the July survey generally indicated that banks eased their lending policies for commercial and industrial (C&I) and CRE loans and experienced stronger demand for such loans over the past three months.[2] In particular, a moderate fraction of domestic respondents reported having eased their standards on C&I loans, and moderate to large net fractions of such respondents reportedly eased many terms on C&I loans to firms of all sizes.[3] Most banks that eased their C&I lending policies cited increased competition for such loans as an important reason for having done so. On net, respondents reported stronger demand for C&I loans over the second quarter, although a few large banks indicated that demand had weakened.[4] A modest net fraction of foreign respondents indicated that they had eased standards on, and a moderate net fraction had experienced stronger demand for, C&I loans in the second quarter.

The survey results also indicated that banks eased standards and terms on, and saw increases in demand for, some categories of lending to households. Modest net fractions of respondents reported having eased standards on prime residential or nontraditional mortgage loans, and a large net fraction indicated that they had seen increased demand for prime mortgage loans. A moderate net fraction of respondents reported that they had eased standards on auto loans over the past three months, and small net fractions indicated that they had eased standards on credit card loans and other consumer loans. Demand for all three types of consumer loans asked about in the survey had reportedly strengthened, on balance, over the second quarter.

---

[1] Respondent banks received the survey on or after July 2, 2013, and responses were due by July 16, 2013.

[2] For questions that ask about lending standards or terms, reported net fractions equal the fraction of banks that reported having tightened standards ("tightened considerably" or "tightened somewhat") minus the fraction of banks that reported having eased standards ("eased considerably" or "eased somewhat"). For questions that ask about demand, reported net fractions equal the fraction of banks that reported stronger demand ("substantially stronger" or "moderately stronger") minus the fraction of banks that reported weaker demand ("substantially weaker" or "moderately weaker").

[3] The survey asks respondents separately about their standards for and demand from large and middle-market firms, which are generally defined as firms with annual sales of $50 million or more, and small firms, those with annual sales of less than $50 million.

[4] Large banks are defined as those with total domestic assets of $20 billion or more as of March 31, 2013.

To complement the usual survey questions about total CRE lending, one set of special questions asked banks separately about changes in standards and demand over the past twelve months for each of the three main categories of CRE loans—construction and land development loans, loans secured by nonfarm nonresidential properties, and loans secured by multifamily residential properties. Banks reported having eased standards on, and having seen increased demand for, all three CRE loan categories over the past twelve months.

The second set of special questions, repeated from the July 2011 and July 2012 surveys, asked about the current levels of banks' lending standards relative to the midpoints of their ranges observed since 2005. Banks generally indicated that standards on C&I loans were currently somewhat easier than the midpoint of that range, while banks' current standards on other categories of business and household loans inquired about were reported to be at least somewhat tighter than the midpoint.

Business Lending
(Table 1, questions 1–14; Table 2, questions 1–14)

Questions on commercial and industrial lending. A moderate fraction of domestic survey respondents, on net, indicated that they had eased their standards for C&I loans to firms of all sizes over the second quarter of 2013. On balance, almost all terms on C&I loans were reportedly eased, regardless of firm size. In particular, sizable net fractions of respondents indicated that they had decreased spreads on C&I loan rates over their bank's cost of funds regardless of firm size. In addition, moderate to large net fractions of banks reported having reduced the cost of credit lines and decreased the use of interest rate floors for all firm sizes.

Of the domestic respondents that reported having eased either standards or terms on C&I loans over the past three months, all but two cited more-aggressive competition from other banks or nonbank lenders as an important reason for having done so. The next most popular reasons indicated by respondents that had eased their C&I loan policies were a more favorable or less uncertain economic outlook, cited by about half of such respondents as being a somewhat important reason, and an increased tolerance for risk, reported by about one-third of such respondents as being a somewhat important or very important reason.

Regarding changes in demand for C&I loans in the second quarter, a moderate net fraction of domestic banks indicated that they had experienced stronger demand from small firms, and a modest net fraction of domestic banks said demand from large and middle-market firms had increased. However, six large banks reported that they had experienced weaker demand from large and middle-market firms. Banks reporting stronger loan demand most often cited increases in customers' funding needs related to investment in plant or equipment, inventories, and accounts receivable as the top reasons. About half of banks experiencing stronger demand also cited shifts in customer borrowing to their bank from other bank or nonbank sources because those sources became less attractive. Banks reporting weaker demand for C&I loans most often cited decreases in customers' funding needs related to merger and acquisition financing, investment in plant or equipment, accounts receivable, or inventories as the top reasons. Slightly more than half of the banks that experienced weaker demand cited increases in their customers' internally generated funds, and about half reported shifts in customers' borrowing away from their bank because other sources of bank or nonbank borrowing became more attractive.

On balance, foreign respondents reported that they had eased their C&I lending standards over the past three months. Banks generally reported that terms on such loans were unchanged, in contrast to the previous three surveys in which they generally reported that they had eased. A moderate net fraction of foreign respondents indicated that demand for C&I loans had strengthened over the second quarter. Most foreign respondents reporting stronger loan demand cited customers' funding needs related to investment in plant or equipment or to merger or acquisition financing as somewhat important reasons.

Questions on commercial real estate lending. A moderate fraction of banks reported that they had eased their standards for approving applications for CRE loans over the second quarter. About half of the banks, on net, reported that they had experienced stronger demand for such loans.

Special questions on commercial real estate lending by loan type. The survey included special questions on changes in standards and demand over the past twelve months for the three major categories of CRE loans—construction and land development loans, loans secured by nonfarm nonresidential properties, and loans secured by multifamily residential properties. Banks reported that they had eased their standards, on balance, on all three types of CRE loans over the past twelve months, though fewer banks so reported for construction and land development loans than for the other two categories of CRE loans. Moderate net fractions indicated that they had experienced stronger demand for all three categories over the same period.

Lending to Households
(Table 1, questions 15–28)

Questions on residential real estate lending. Modest net fractions of domestic respondents to the July survey reported that they had eased standards on prime residential or nontraditional mortgage loans over the past three months. A large net fraction of banks reported having experienced stronger demand for prime residential mortgages, but demand for nontraditional mortgages reportedly weakened. Banks reported that their standards on home equity lines of credit were little changed, and a modest net fraction of banks indicated that they had seen increased demand for those products.

Questions on consumer lending. Responses from domestic banks indicated that they were somewhat more willing to make consumer installment loans than three months previously. However, while a moderate net fraction of banks reported having eased standards on auto loans, only small net fractions indicated that they had eased standards on credit card loans and other consumer loans. On balance, banks reported reducing spreads on auto loans, increasing the maximum maturity on auto loans, and easing credit limits on credit cards. Other terms across the three categories of consumer loans remained little changed, on net, over the past three months. A moderate net fraction of banks reported having experienced increased demand for auto loans; smaller net fractions indicated they had seen stronger demand for credit card loans and other consumer loans.

Special questions on the levels of lending standards relative to longer-term norms.
(Table 1, question 29; Table 2, question 15)

The July survey repeated a set of special questions from July 2011 and July 2012 that asked respondents to describe the current level of lending standards at their bank, rather than changes in standards over the survey period. Specifically, for each loan category surveyed, banks were asked to consider the range over which their bank's standards have varied between 2005 and the present and to report where the current level of standards for such loans resides relative to the midpoint of that range.

Regarding loans to businesses, moderate net fractions of domestic banks reported that lending standards on four different kinds of C&I loans (investment-grade syndicated loans, below-investment-grade syndicated loans, other loans to large and middle-market firms, and loans to small firms) were currently at levels that were easier than the midpoints of the ranges that those standards have occupied since 2005. Foreign banks generally reported that the levels of standards on loans to large firms were easier than the midpoints, while standards on loans to small firms were reported to be about at the midpoint. Modest to moderate net fractions of domestic banks reported that the current standards on all types of CRE loans (construction and land development loans; loans secured by nonfarm, nonresidential structures; and loans secured by multifamily structures) were tighter than the midpoints of the ranges that those standards have occupied since 2005. Compared with the results in the July 2012 survey, these results for all types of C&I and CRE loans indicate some easing of credit conditions from the levels reported a year ago.

With respect to loans to households, moderate to large net fractions of banks reported that lending standards for all six categories of residential mortgages included in the survey (prime conforming mortgages, mortgages guaranteed by the Federal Housing Administration or the U.S. Department of Veterans Affairs, prime jumbo mortgages, subprime mortgages, nontraditional mortgages, and HELOCs) remained at least somewhat tighter than the midpoints of the ranges that those standards have occupied since 2005. Modest net fractions of domestic banks reported that standards were tighter than the midpoint for prime credit card, subprime credit card, auto, and other consumer loans. Compared with the results in the July 2012 survey, lending standards for many types of household loans appear to be little changed.

This document was prepared by John C. Driscoll and Vladimir Yankov, with the assistance of Shaily Patel, Division of Monetary Affairs, Board of Governors of the Federal Reserve System.

Measures of Supply and Demand for Commercial and Industrial Loans, by Size of Firm Seeking Loan

Net Percentage of Domestic Respondents Tightening Standards for Commercial and Industrial Loans

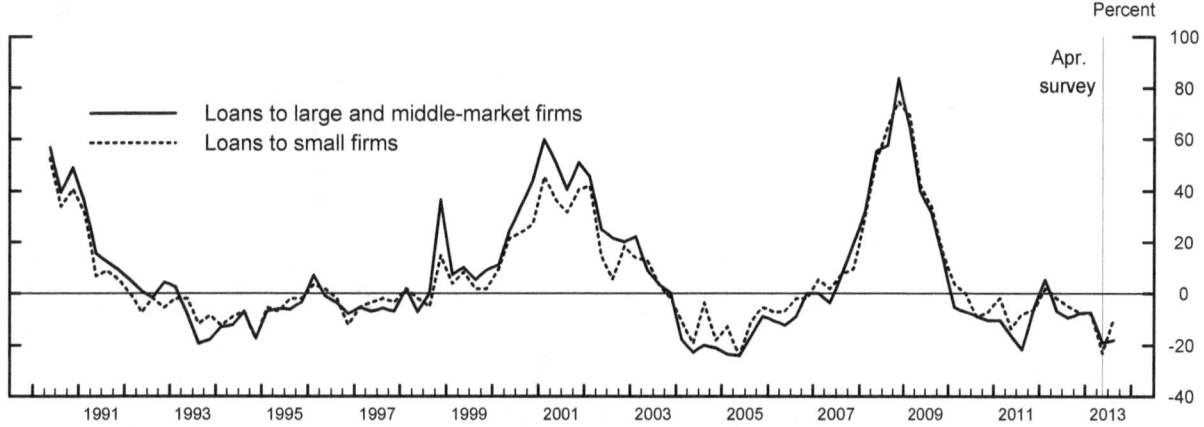

Net Percentage of Domestic Respondents Increasing Spreads of Loan Rates over Bank's Cost of Funds

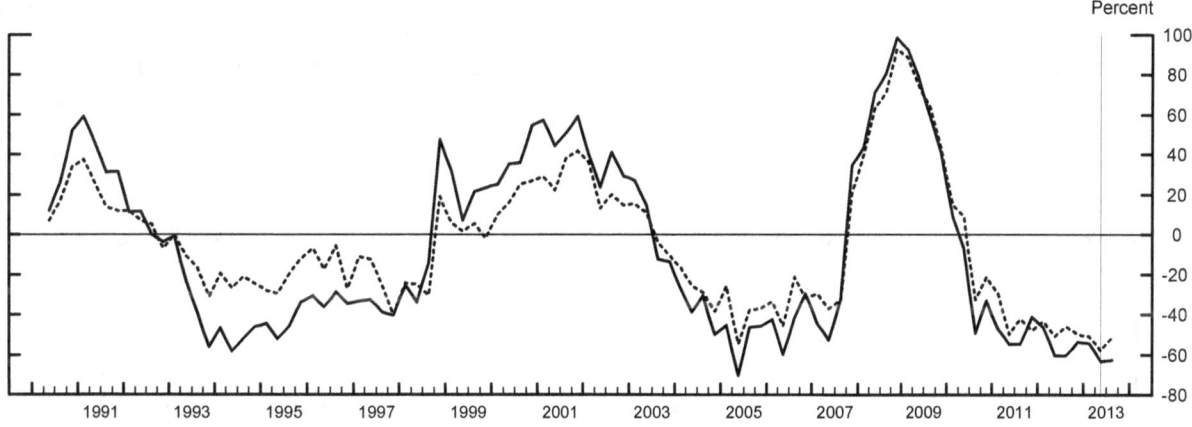

Net Percentage of Domestic Respondents Reporting Stronger Demand for Commercial and Industrial Loans

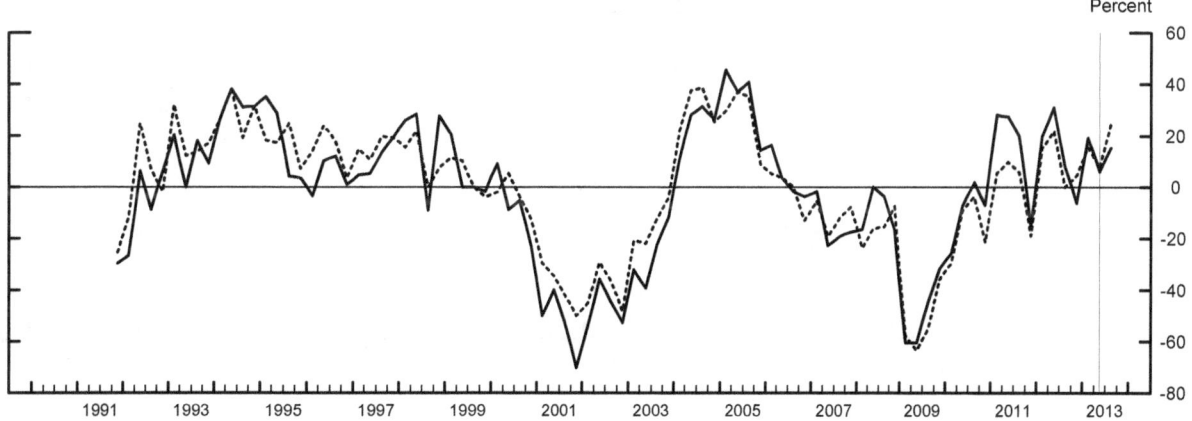

Measures of Supply and Demand for Commercial Real Estate Loans

Net Percentage of Domestic Respondents Tightening Standards for Commercial Real Estate Loans

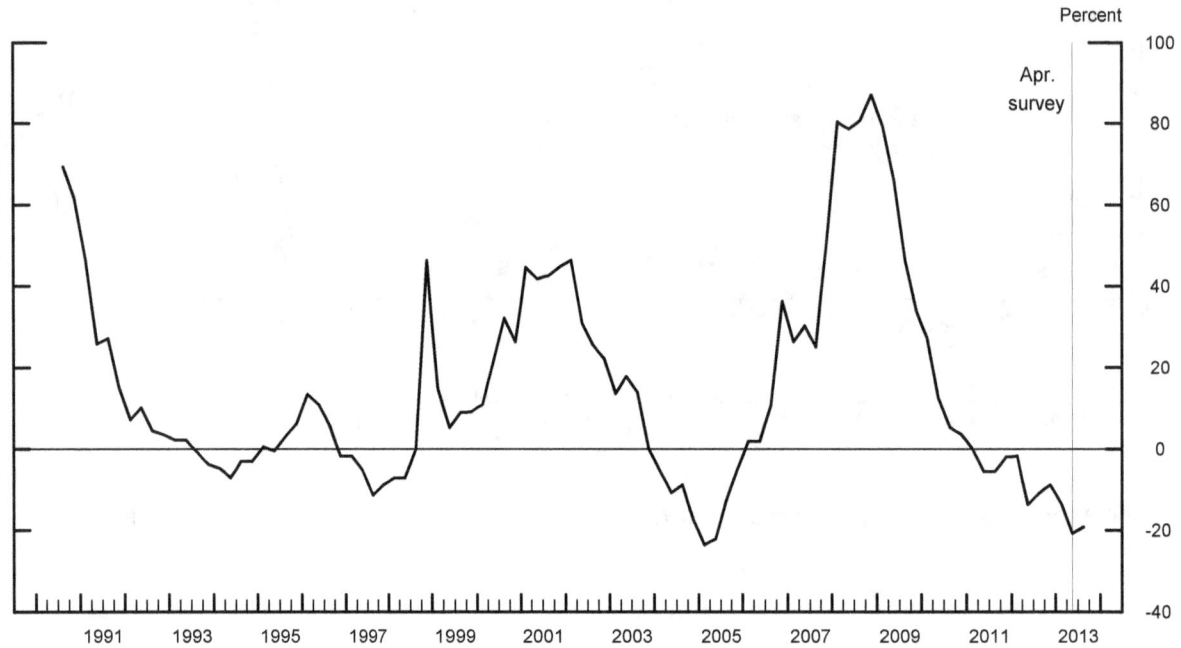

Net Percentage of Domestic Respondents Reporting Stronger Demand for Commercial Real Estate Loans

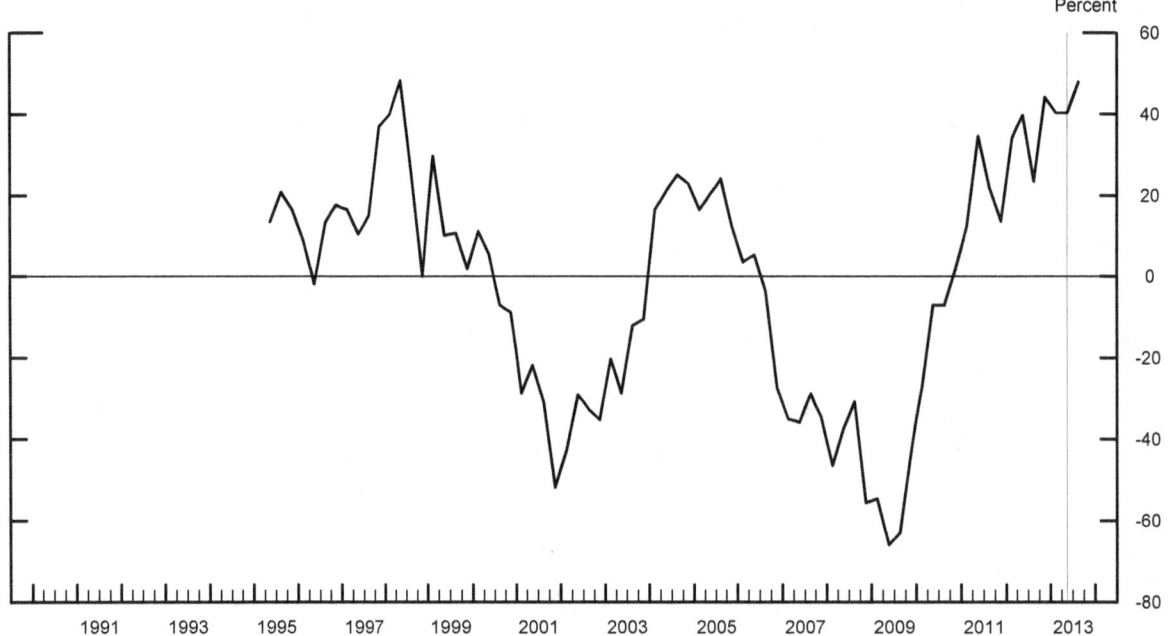

Measures of Supply and Demand for Residential Mortgage Loans

Net Percentage of Domestic Respondents Tightening Standards for Residential Mortgage Loans

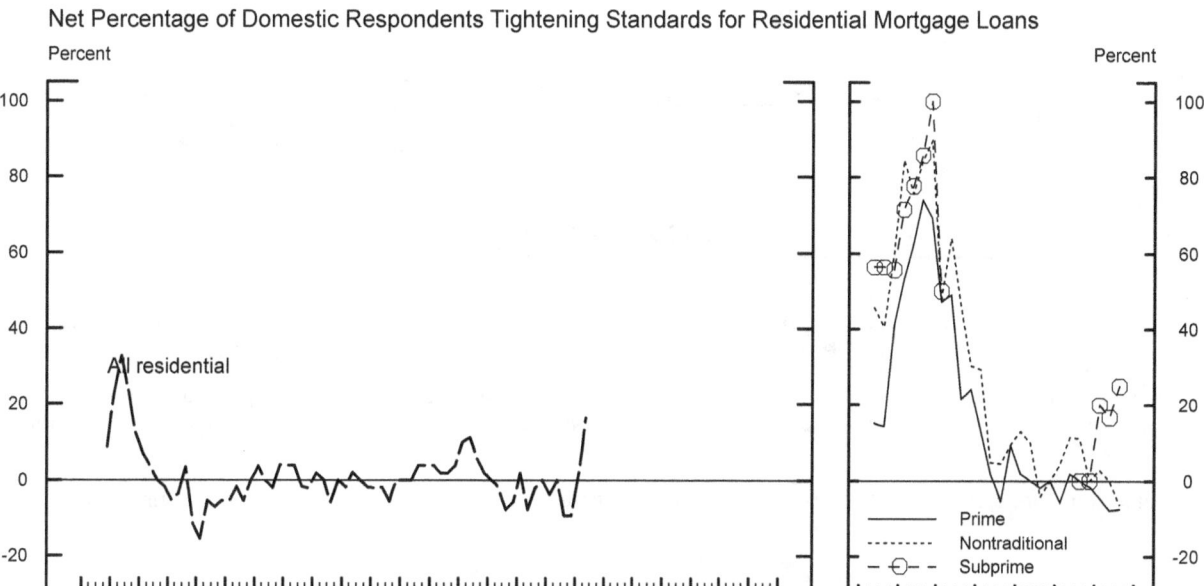

Note: For data starting in 2007:Q2, changes in standards for prime, nontraditional, and subprime mortgage loans are reported separately. Series are not reported when he number of respondents is three or fewer.

Net Percentage of Domestic Respondents Reporting Stronger Demand for Residential Mortgage Loans

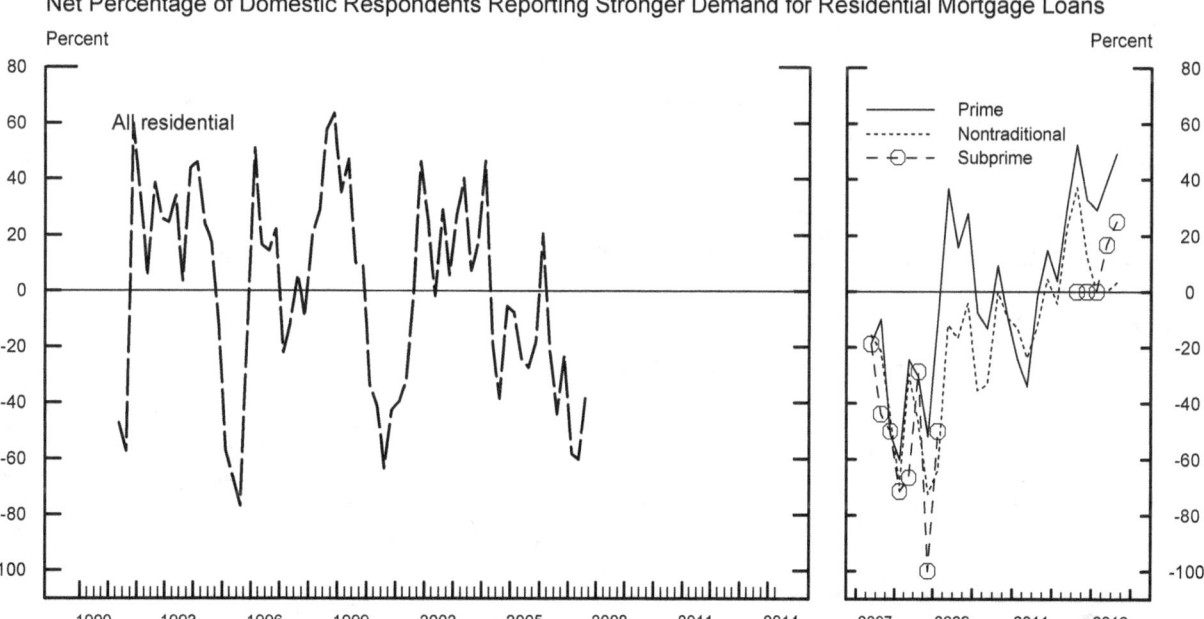

Note: For data starting in 2007:Q2, changes in demand for prime, nontraditional, and subprime mortgage loans are reported separately. Series are not reported when he number of respondents is three or fewer.

Measures of Supply and Demand for Consumer Loans

Net Percentage of Domestic Respondents Tightening Standards for Consumer Loans

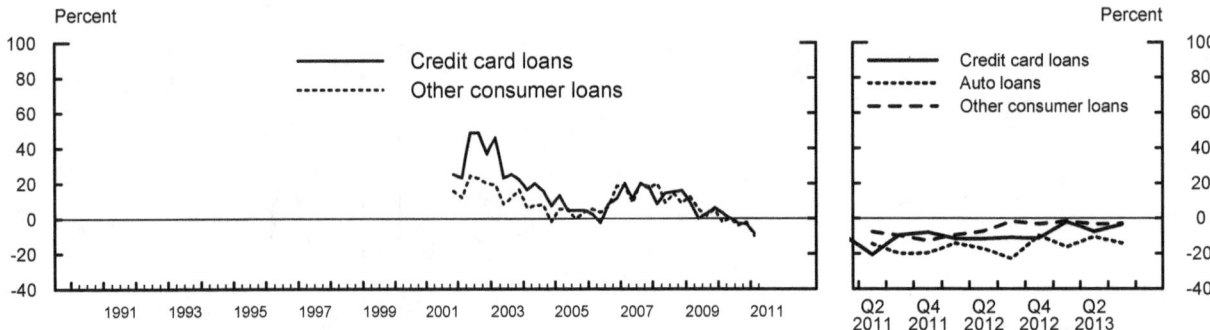

Note: For data starting in 2011:Q2, changes in standards for auto loans and consumer loans excluding credit card and auto loans are reported separately. In 2011:Q2 only, new and used auto loans are reported separately and equally weighted to calculate the auto loans series.

Net Percentage of Domestic Respondents Reporting Increased Willingness to Make Consumer Installment Loans

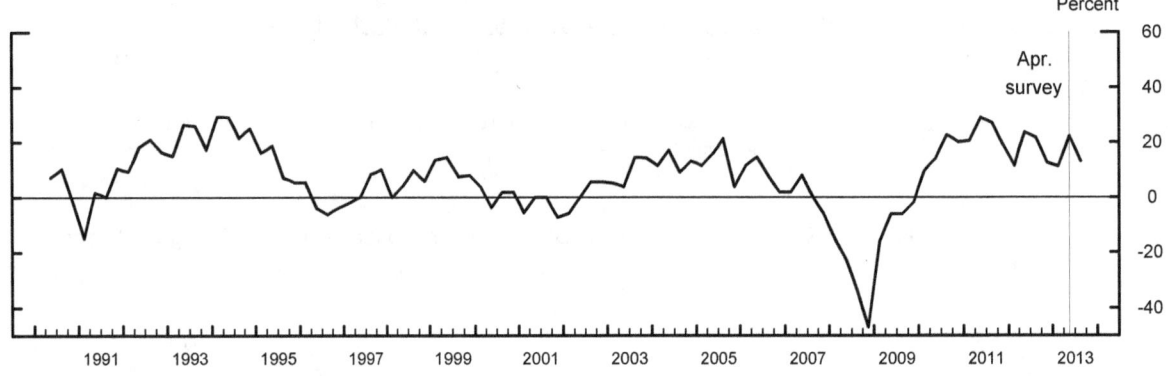

Net Percentage of Domestic Respondents Reporting Stronger Demand for Consumer Loans

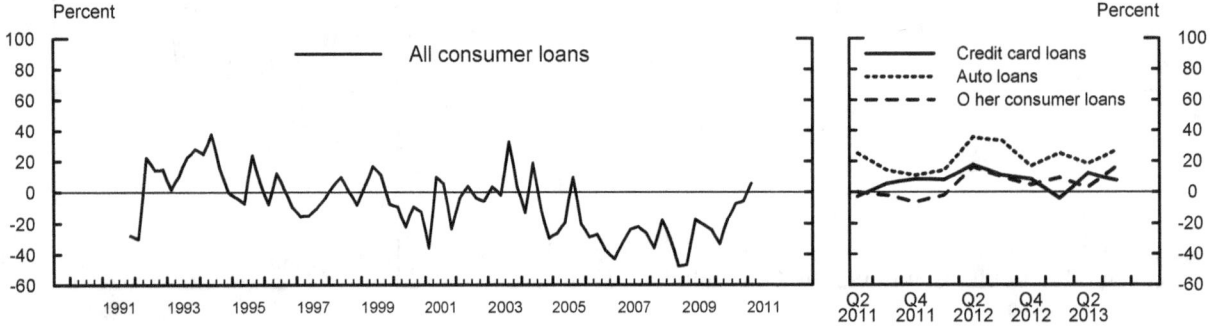

Note: For data starting in 2011:Q2, changes in demand for credit card loans, auto loans, and consumer loans excluding credit card and auto loans are reported separately.

Table 1

Senior Loan Officer Opinion Survey on Bank Lending Practices at Selected Large Banks in the United States [1]

(Status of policy as of July 2013)

Questions 1-6 *ask about commercial and industrial (C&I) loans at your bank. Questions 1-3 deal with changes in your bank's lending policies over the past three months. Questions 4-5 deal with changes in demand for C&I loans over the past three months. Question 6 asks about changes in prospective demand for C&I loans at your bank, as indicated by the volume of recent inquiries about the availability of new credit lines or increases in existing lines. If your bank's lending policies have not changed over the past three months, please report them as unchanged even if the policies are either restrictive or accommodative relative to longer-term norms. If your bank's policies have tightened or eased over the past three months, please so report them regardless of how they stand relative to longer-term norms. Also, please report changes in enforcement of existing policies as changes in policies.*

1. Over the past three months, how have your bank's credit standards for approving applications for C&I loans or credit lines—other than those to be used to finance mergers and acquisitions—to large and middle-market firms and to small firms changed? (If your bank defines firm size differently from the categories suggested below, please use your definitions and indicate what they are.)

A. Standards for large and middle-market firms (annual sales of $50 million or more):

	All Respondents		Large Banks		Other Banks	
	Banks	Percent	Banks	Percent	Banks	Percent
Tightened considerably	0	0.0	0	0.0	0	0.0
Tightened somewhat	1	1.4	0	0.0	1	2.9
Remained basically unchanged	57	79.2	29	76.3	28	82.4
Eased somewhat	13	18.1	9	23.7	4	11.8
Eased considerably	1	1.4	0	0.0	1	2.9
Total	72	100.0	38	100.0	34	100.0

B. Standards for small firms (annual sales of less than $50 million):

	All Respondents		Large Banks		Other Banks	
	Banks	Percent	Banks	Percent	Banks	Percent
Tightened considerably	0	0.0	0	0.0	0	0.0
Tightened somewhat	0	0.0	0	0.0	0	0.0
Remained basically unchanged	63	90.0	33	94.3	30	85.7
Eased somewhat	7	10.0	2	5.7	5	14.3
Eased considerably	0	0.0	0	0.0	0	0.0
Total	70	100.0	35	100.0	35	100.0

2. For applications for C&I loans or credit lines—other than those to be used to finance mergers and acquisitions—from large and middle-market firms and from small firms that your bank currently is willing to approve, how have the terms of those loans changed over the past three months?

A. Terms for large and middle-market firms (annual sales of $50 million or more):

a. Maximum size of credit lines

	All Respondents		Large Banks		Other Banks	
	Banks	Percent	Banks	Percent	Banks	Percent
Tightened considerably	0	0.0	0	0.0	0	0.0
Tightened somewhat	0	0.0	0	0.0	0	0.0
Remained basically unchanged	59	83.1	29	78.4	30	88.2
Eased somewhat	11	15.5	8	21.6	3	8.8
Eased considerably	1	1.4	0	0.0	1	2.9
Total	71	100.0	37	100.0	34	100.0

b. Maximum maturity of loans or credit lines

	All Respondents		Large Banks		Other Banks	
	Banks	Percent	Banks	Percent	Banks	Percent
Tightened considerably	0	0.0	0	0.0	0	0.0
Tightened somewhat	0	0.0	0	0.0	0	0.0
Remained basically unchanged	63	87.5	36	94.7	27	79.4
Eased somewhat	9	12.5	2	5.3	7	20.6
Eased considerably	0	0.0	0	0.0	0	0.0
Total	72	100.0	38	100.0	34	100.0

c. Costs of credit lines

	All Respondents		Large Banks		Other Banks	
	Banks	Percent	Banks	Percent	Banks	Percent
Tightened considerably	0	0.0	0	0.0	0	0.0
Tightened somewhat	0	0.0	0	0.0	0	0.0
Remained basically unchanged	39	54.2	23	60.5	16	47.1
Eased somewhat	32	44.4	15	39.5	17	50.0
Eased considerably	1	1.4	0	0.0	1	2.9
Total	72	100.0	38	100.0	34	100.0

d. Spreads of loan rates over your bank's cost of funds (wider spreads=tightened, narrower spreads=eased)

	All Respondents		Large Banks		Other Banks	
	Banks	Percent	Banks	Percent	Banks	Percent
Tightened considerably	0	0.0	0	0.0	0	0.0
Tightened somewhat	3	4.2	1	2.6	2	5.9
Remained basically unchanged	21	29.2	11	28.9	10	29.4
Eased somewhat	48	66.7	26	68.4	22	64.7
Eased considerably	0	0.0	0	0.0	0	0.0
Total	72	100.0	38	100.0	34	100.0

e. Premiums charged on riskier loans

	All Respondents		Large Banks		Other Banks	
	Banks	Percent	Banks	Percent	Banks	Percent
Tightened considerably	1	1.4	1	2.6	0	0.0
Tightened somewhat	3	4.2	0	0.0	3	8.8
Remained basically unchanged	57	79.2	29	76.3	28	82.4
Eased somewhat	10	13.9	7	18.4	3	8.8
Eased considerably	1	1.4	1	2.6	0	0.0
Total	72	100.0	38	100.0	34	100.0

f. Loan covenants

	All Respondents		Large Banks		Other Banks	
	Banks	Percent	Banks	Percent	Banks	Percent
Tightened considerably	0	0.0	0	0.0	0	0.0
Tightened somewhat	2	2.8	1	2.6	1	2.9
Remained basically unchanged	49	68.1	21	55.3	28	82.4
Eased somewhat	20	27.8	16	42.1	4	11.8
Eased considerably	1	1.4	0	0.0	1	2.9
Total	72	100.0	38	100.0	34	100.0

g. Collateralization requirements

	All Respondents		Large Banks		Other Banks	
	Banks	Percent	Banks	Percent	Banks	Percent
Tightened considerably	0	0.0	0	0.0	0	0.0
Tightened somewhat	0	0.0	0	0.0	0	0.0
Remained basically unchanged	71	98.6	37	97.4	34	100.0
Eased somewhat	1	1.4	1	2.6	0	0.0
Eased considerably	0	0.0	0	0.0	0	0.0
Total	72	100.0	38	100.0	34	100.0

h. Use of interest rate floors (more use=tightened, less use=eased)

	All Respondents		Large Banks		Other Banks	
	Banks	Percent	Banks	Percent	Banks	Percent
Tightened considerably	0	0.0	0	0.0	0	0.0
Tightened somewhat	1	1.4	0	0.0	1	2.9
Remained basically unchanged	41	58.6	23	63.9	18	52.9
Eased somewhat	23	32.9	10	27.8	13	38.2
Eased considerably	5	7.1	3	8.3	2	5.9
Total	70	100.0	36	100.0	34	100.0

B. Terms for small firms (annual sales of less than $50 million):

a. Maximum size of credit lines

	All Respondents		Large Banks		Other Banks	
	Banks	Percent	Banks	Percent	Banks	Percent
Tightened considerably	0	0.0	0	0.0	0	0.0
Tightened somewhat	0	0.0	0	0.0	0	0.0
Remained basically unchanged	63	90.0	32	91.4	31	88.6
Eased somewhat	6	8.6	3	8.6	3	8.6
Eased considerably	1	1.4	0	0.0	1	2.9
Total	70	100.0	35	100.0	35	100.0

b. Maximum maturity of loans or credit lines

	All Respondents		Large Banks		Other Banks	
	Banks	Percent	Banks	Percent	Banks	Percent
Tightened considerably	0	0.0	0	0.0	0	0.0
Tightened somewhat	0	0.0	0	0.0	0	0.0
Remained basically unchanged	59	84.3	29	82.9	30	85.7
Eased somewhat	11	15.7	6	17.1	5	14.3
Eased considerably	0	0.0	0	0.0	0	0.0
Total	70	100.0	35	100.0	35	100.0

c. Costs of credit lines

	All Respondents		Large Banks		Other Banks	
	Banks	Percent	Banks	Percent	Banks	Percent
Tightened considerably	0	0.0	0	0.0	0	0.0
Tightened somewhat	0	0.0	0	0.0	0	0.0
Remained basically unchanged	44	62.9	25	71.4	19	54.3
Eased somewhat	26	37.1	10	28.6	16	45.7
Eased considerably	0	0.0	0	0.0	0	0.0
Total	70	100.0	35	100.0	35	100.0

d. Spreads of loan rates over your bank's cost of funds (wider spreads=tightened, narrower spreads=eased)

	All Respondents		Large Banks		Other Banks	
	Banks	Percent	Banks	Percent	Banks	Percent
Tightened considerably	0	0.0	0	0.0	0	0.0
Tightened somewhat	4	5.7	2	5.7	2	5.7
Remained basically unchanged	26	37.1	13	37.1	13	37.1
Eased somewhat	40	57.1	20	57.1	20	57.1
Eased considerably	0	0.0	0	0.0	0	0.0
Total	70	100.0	35	100.0	35	100.0

e. Premiums charged on riskier loans

	All Respondents		Large Banks		Other Banks	
	Banks	Percent	Banks	Percent	Banks	Percent
Tightened considerably	0	0.0	0	0.0	0	0.0
Tightened somewhat	2	2.9	0	0.0	2	5.7
Remained basically unchanged	61	87.1	31	88.6	30	85.7
Eased somewhat	5	7.1	3	8.6	2	5.7
Eased considerably	2	2.9	1	2.9	1	2.9
Total	70	100.0	35	100.0	35	100.0

f. Loan covenants

	All Respondents		Large Banks		Other Banks	
	Banks	Percent	Banks	Percent	Banks	Percent
Tightened considerably	0	0.0	0	0.0	0	0.0
Tightened somewhat	2	2.9	0	0.0	2	5.7
Remained basically unchanged	57	81.4	26	74.3	31	88.6
Eased somewhat	11	15.7	9	25.7	2	5.7
Eased considerably	0	0.0	0	0.0	0	0.0
Total	70	100.0	35	100.0	35	100.0

g. Collateralization requirements

	All Respondents		Large Banks		Other Banks	
	Banks	Percent	Banks	Percent	Banks	Percent
Tightened considerably	0	0.0	0	0.0	0	0.0
Tightened somewhat	0	0.0	0	0.0	0	0.0
Remained basically unchanged	68	97.1	34	97.1	34	97.1
Eased somewhat	2	2.9	1	2.9	1	2.9
Eased considerably	0	0.0	0	0.0	0	0.0
Total	70	100.0	35	100.0	35	100.0

h. Use of interest rate floors (more use=tightened, less use=eased)

	All Respondents		Large Banks		Other Banks	
	Banks	Percent	Banks	Percent	Banks	Percent
Tightened considerably	0	0.0	0	0.0	0	0.0
Tightened somewhat	1	1.4	0	0.0	1	2.9
Remained basically unchanged	47	68.1	26	76.5	21	60.0
Eased somewhat	17	24.6	6	17.6	11	31.4
Eased considerably	4	5.8	2	5.9	2	5.7
Total	69	100.0	34	100.0	35	100.0

3. If your bank has tightened or eased its credit standards or its terms for C&I loans or credit lines over the past three months (as described in questions 1 and 2), how important have been the following possible reasons for the change?

A. Possible reasons for tightening credit standards or loan terms:

a. Deterioration in your bank's current or expected capital position

	All Respondents		Large Banks		Other Banks	
	Banks	Percent	Banks	Percent	Banks	Percent
Not important	6	85.7	3	100.0	3	75.0
Somewhat important	0	0.0	0	0.0	0	0.0
Very important	1	14.3	0	0.0	1	25.0
Total	7	100.0	3	100.0	4	100.0

b. Less favorable or more uncertain economic outlook

	All Respondents		Large Banks		Other Banks	
	Banks	Percent	Banks	Percent	Banks	Percent
Not important	3	42.9	2	66.7	1	25.0
Somewhat important	2	28.6	0	0.0	2	50.0
Very important	2	28.6	1	33.3	1	25.0
Total	7	100.0	3	100.0	4	100.0

c. Worsening of industry-specific problems (please specify industries)

	All Respondents		Large Banks		Other Banks	
	Banks	Percent	Banks	Percent	Banks	Percent
Not important	5	71.4	3	100.0	2	50.0
Somewhat important	1	14.3	0	0.0	1	25.0
Very important	1	14.3	0	0.0	1	25.0
Total	7	100.0	3	100.0	4	100.0

d. Less aggressive competition from other banks or nonbank lenders (other financial intermediaries or the capital markets)

	All Respondents		Large Banks		Other Banks	
	Banks	Percent	Banks	Percent	Banks	Percent
Not important	6	85.7	3	100.0	3	75.0
Somewhat important	0	0.0	0	0.0	0	0.0
Very important	1	14.3	0	0.0	1	25.0
Total	7	100.0	3	100.0	4	100.0

e. Reduced tolerance for risk

	All Respondents		Large Banks		Other Banks	
	Banks	Percent	Banks	Percent	Banks	Percent
Not important	3	42.9	3	100.0	0	0.0
Somewhat important	2	28.6	0	0.0	2	50.0
Very important	2	28.6	0	0.0	2	50.0
Total	7	100.0	3	100.0	4	100.0

f. Decreased liquidity in the secondary market for these loans

	All Respondents		Large Banks		Other Banks	
	Banks	Percent	Banks	Percent	Banks	Percent
Not important	4	57.1	2	66.7	2	50.0
Somewhat important	3	42.9	1	33.3	2	50.0
Very important	0	0.0	0	0.0	0	0.0
Total	7	100.0	3	100.0	4	100.0

g. Deterioration in your bank's current or expected liquidity position

	All Respondents		Large Banks		Other Banks	
	Banks	Percent	Banks	Percent	Banks	Percent
Not important	6	85.7	3	100.0	3	75.0
Somewhat important	0	0.0	0	0.0	0	0.0
Very important	1	14.3	0	0.0	1	25.0
Total	7	100.0	3	100.0	4	100.0

h. Increased concerns about the effects of legislative changes, supervisory actions, or changes in accounting standards

	All Respondents		Large Banks		Other Banks	
	Banks	Percent	Banks	Percent	Banks	Percent
Not important	4	57.1	3	100.0	1	25.0
Somewhat important	2	28.6	0	0.0	2	50.0
Very important	1	14.3	0	0.0	1	25.0
Total	7	100.0	3	100.0	4	100.0

B. Possible reasons for easing credit standards or loan terms:

a. Improvement in your bank's current or expected capital position

	All Respondents		Large Banks		Other Banks	
	Banks	Percent	Banks	Percent	Banks	Percent
Not important	45	90.0	24	88.9	21	91.3
Somewhat important	3	6.0	2	7.4	1	4.3
Very important	2	4.0	1	3.7	1	4.3
Total	50	100.0	27	100.0	23	100.0

b. More favorable or less uncertain economic outlook

	All Respondents		Large Banks		Other Banks	
	Banks	Percent	Banks	Percent	Banks	Percent
Not important	25	49.0	13	48.1	12	50.0
Somewhat important	26	51.0	14	51.9	12	50.0
Very important	0	0.0	0	0.0	0	0.0
Total	51	100.0	27	100.0	24	100.0

c. Improvement in industry-specific problems (please specify industries)

	All Respondents		Large Banks		Other Banks	
	Banks	Percent	Banks	Percent	Banks	Percent
Not important	41	85.4	24	96.0	17	73.9
Somewhat important	5	10.4	1	4.0	4	17.4
Very important	2	4.2	0	0.0	2	8.7
Total	48	100.0	25	100.0	23	100.0

d. More aggressive competition from other banks or nonbank lenders (other financial intermediaries or the capital markets)

	All Respondents		Large Banks		Other Banks	
	Banks	Percent	Banks	Percent	Banks	Percent
Not important	2	3.9	2	7.4	0	0.0
Somewhat important	13	25.5	4	14.8	9	37.5
Very important	36	70.6	21	77.8	15	62.5
Total	51	100.0	27	100.0	24	100.0

e. Increased tolerance for risk

	All Respondents		Large Banks		Other Banks	
	Banks	Percent	Banks	Percent	Banks	Percent
Not important	35	70.0	22	81.5	13	56.5
Somewhat important	14	28.0	5	18.5	9	39.1
Very important	1	2.0	0	0.0	1	4.3
Total	50	100.0	27	100.0	23	100.0

f. Increased liquidity in the secondary market for these loans

	All Respondents		Large Banks		Other Banks	
	Banks	Percent	Banks	Percent	Banks	Percent
Not important	38	76.0	19	70.4	19	82.6
Somewhat important	9	18.0	7	25.9	2	8.7
Very important	3	6.0	1	3.7	2	8.7
Total	50	100.0	27	100.0	23	100.0

g. Improvement in your bank's current or expected liquidity position

	All Respondents		Large Banks		Other Banks	
	Banks	Percent	Banks	Percent	Banks	Percent
Not important	40	78.4	25	92.6	15	62.5
Somewhat important	10	19.6	2	7.4	8	33.3
Very important	1	2.0	0	0.0	1	4.2
Total	51	100.0	27	100.0	24	100.0

h. Reduced concerns about the effects of legislative changes, supervisory actions, or changes in accounting standards

	All Respondents		Large Banks		Other Banks	
	Banks	Percent	Banks	Percent	Banks	Percent
Not important	45	90.0	24	88.9	21	91.3
Somewhat important	4	8.0	3	11.1	1	4.3
Very important	1	2.0	0	0.0	1	4.3
Total	50	100.0	27	100.0	23	100.0

4. Apart from normal seasonal variation, how has demand for C&I loans changed over the past three months? (Please consider only funds actually disbursed as opposed to requests for new or increased lines of credit.)

A. Demand for C&I loans from large and middle-market firms (annual sales of $50 million or more):

	All Respondents		Large Banks		Other Banks	
	Banks	Percent	Banks	Percent	Banks	Percent
Substantially stronger	0	0.0	0	0.0	0	0.0
Moderately stronger	20	27.8	9	23.7	11	32.4
About the same	43	59.7	23	60.5	20	58.8
Moderately weaker	9	12.5	6	15.8	3	8.8
Substantially weaker	0	0.0	0	0.0	0	0.0
Total	72	100.0	38	100.0	34	100.0

B. Demand for C&I loans from small firms (annual sales of less than $50 million):

	All Respondents		Large Banks		Other Banks	
	Banks	Percent	Banks	Percent	Banks	Percent
Substantially stronger	1	1.4	0	0.0	1	2.9
Moderately stronger	21	30.0	8	22.9	13	37.1
About the same	43	61.4	25	71.4	18	51.4
Moderately weaker	5	7.1	2	5.7	3	8.6
Substantially weaker	0	0.0	0	0.0	0	0.0
Total	70	100.0	35	100.0	35	100.0

5. If demand for C&I loans has strengthened or weakened over the past three months (as described in question 4), how important have been the following possible reasons for the change?

A. If stronger loan demand (answer 1 or 2 to question 4A or 4B), possible reasons:

a. Customer inventory financing needs increased

	All Respondents		Large Banks		Other Banks	
	Banks	Percent	Banks	Percent	Banks	Percent
Not important	6	23.1	4	33.3	2	14.3
Somewhat important	20	76.9	8	66.7	12	85.7
Very important	0	0.0	0	0.0	0	0.0
Total	26	100.0	12	100.0	14	100.0

b. Customer accounts receivable financing needs increased

	All Respondents		Large Banks		Other Banks	
	Banks	Percent	Banks	Percent	Banks	Percent
Not important	3	11.5	2	16.7	1	7.1
Somewhat important	23	88.5	10	83.3	13	92.9
Very important	0	0.0	0	0.0	0	0.0
Total	26	100.0	12	100.0	14	100.0

c. Customer investment in plant or equipment increased

	All Respondents		Large Banks		Other Banks	
	Banks	Percent	Banks	Percent	Banks	Percent
Not important	2	7.7	2	16.7	0	0.0
Somewhat important	23	88.5	10	83.3	13	92.9
Very important	1	3.8	0	0.0	1	7.1
Total	26	100.0	12	100.0	14	100.0

d. Customer internally generated funds decreased

	All Respondents		Large Banks		Other Banks	
	Banks	Percent	Banks	Percent	Banks	Percent
Not important	23	92.0	11	91.7	12	92.3
Somewhat important	2	8.0	1	8.3	1	7.7
Very important	0	0.0	0	0.0	0	0.0
Total	25	100.0	12	100.0	13	100.0

e. Customer merger or acquisition financing needs increased

	All Respondents		Large Banks		Other Banks	
	Banks	Percent	Banks	Percent	Banks	Percent
Not important	9	36.0	3	25.0	6	46.2
Somewhat important	14	56.0	8	66.7	6	46.2
Very important	2	8.0	1	8.3	1	7.7
Total	25	100.0	12	100.0	13	100.0

f. Customer borrowing shifted to your bank from other bank or nonbank sources because these other sources became less attractive

	All Respondents		Large Banks		Other Banks	
	Banks	Percent	Banks	Percent	Banks	Percent
Not important	12	46.2	5	41.7	7	50.0
Somewhat important	8	30.8	5	41.7	3	21.4
Very important	6	23.1	2	16.7	4	28.6
Total	26	100.0	12	100.0	14	100.0

g. Customers' precautionary demand for cash and liquidity increased

	All Respondents		Large Banks		Other Banks	
	Banks	Percent	Banks	Percent	Banks	Percent
Not important	20	80.0	9	75.0	11	84.6
Somewhat important	5	20.0	3	25.0	2	15.4
Very important	0	0.0	0	0.0	0	0.0
Total	25	100.0	12	100.0	13	100.0

h. Customers transitioned from commercial real estate loans to C&I loans

	All Respondents		Large Banks		Other Banks	
	Banks	Percent	Banks	Percent	Banks	Percent
Not important	22	88.0	10	83.3	12	92.3
Somewhat important	3	12.0	2	16.7	1	7.7
Very important	0	0.0	0	0.0	0	0.0
Total	25	100.0	12	100.0	13	100.0

B. If weaker loan demand (answer 4 or 5 to question 4A or 4B), possible reasons:

a. Customer inventory financing needs decreased

	All Respondents		Large Banks		Other Banks	
	Banks	Percent	Banks	Percent	Banks	Percent
Not important	4	44.4	3	50.0	1	33.3
Somewhat important	4	44.4	2	33.3	2	66.7
Very important	1	11.1	1	16.7	0	0.0
Total	9	100.0	6	100.0	3	100.0

b. Customer accounts receivable financing needs decreased

	All Respondents		Large Banks		Other Banks	
	Banks	Percent	Banks	Percent	Banks	Percent
Not important	4	44.4	3	50.0	1	33.3
Somewhat important	4	44.4	2	33.3	2	66.7
Very important	1	11.1	1	16.7	0	0.0
Total	9	100.0	6	100.0	3	100.0

c. Customer investment in plant or equipment decreased

	All Respondents		Large Banks		Other Banks	
	Banks	Percent	Banks	Percent	Banks	Percent
Not important	3	33.3	3	50.0	0	0.0
Somewhat important	5	55.6	2	33.3	3	100.0
Very important	1	11.1	1	16.7	0	0.0
Total	9	100.0	6	100.0	3	100.0

d. Customer internally generated funds increased

	All Respondents		Large Banks		Other Banks	
	Banks	Percent	Banks	Percent	Banks	Percent
Not important	4	44.4	1	16.7	3	100.0
Somewhat important	4	44.4	4	66.7	0	0.0
Very important	1	11.1	1	16.7	0	0.0
Total	9	100.0	6	100.0	3	100.0

e. Customer merger or acquisition financing needs decreased

	All Respondents		Large Banks		Other Banks	
	Banks	Percent	Banks	Percent	Banks	Percent
Not important	2	22.2	1	16.7	1	33.3
Somewhat important	5	55.6	3	50.0	2	66.7
Very important	2	22.2	2	33.3	0	0.0
Total	9	100.0	6	100.0	3	100.0

f. Customer borrowing shifted from your bank to other bank or nonbank sources because these other sources became more attractive

	All Respondents		Large Banks		Other Banks	
	Banks	Percent	Banks	Percent	Banks	Percent
Not important	4	50.0	3	60.0	1	33.3
Somewhat important	2	25.0	1	20.0	1	33.3
Very important	2	25.0	1	20.0	1	33.3
Total	8	100.0	5	100.0	3	100.0

g. Customers' precautionary demand for cash and liquidity decreased

	All Respondents		Large Banks		Other Banks	
	Banks	Percent	Banks	Percent	Banks	Percent
Not important	6	75.0	3	60.0	3	100.0
Somewhat important	2	25.0	2	40.0	0	0.0
Very important	0	0.0	0	0.0	0	0.0
Total	8	100.0	5	100.0	3	100.0

h. Customers transitioned from C&I loans to commercial real estate loans

	All Respondents		Large Banks		Other Banks	
	Banks	Percent	Banks	Percent	Banks	Percent
Not important	8	100.0	5	100.0	3	100.0
Somewhat important	0	0.0	0	0.0	0	0.0
Very important	0	0.0	0	0.0	0	0.0
Total	8	100.0	5	100.0	3	100.0

6. At your bank, apart from seasonal variation, how has the number of inquiries from potential business borrowers regarding the availability and terms of new credit lines or increases in existing lines changed over the past three months? (Please consider only inquiries for additional or increased C&I lines as opposed to the refinancing of existing loans.)

	All Respondents		Large Banks		Other Banks	
	Banks	Percent	Banks	Percent	Banks	Percent
The number of inquiries has increased substantially	1	1.4	0	0.0	1	2.9
The number of inquiries has increased moderately	28	38.4	13	34.2	15	42.9
The number of inquiries has stayed about the same	38	52.1	21	55.3	17	48.6
The number of inquiries has decreased moderately	6	8.2	4	10.5	2	5.7
The number of inquiries has decreased substantially	0	0.0	0	0.0	0	0.0
Total	73	100.0	38	100.0	35	100.0

Questions 7-8 ask about commercial real estate (CRE) loans at your bank, including construction and land development loans and loans secured by nonfarm nonresidential real estate. Question 7 deals with changes in your bank's standards over the past three months. Question 8 deals with changes in demand. If your bank's lending standards or terms have not changed over the relevant period, please report them as unchanged even if they are either restrictive or accommodative relative to longer-term norms. If your bank's standards or terms have tightened or eased over the relevant period, please so report them regardless of how they stand relative to longer-term norms. Also, please report changes in enforcement of existing standards as changes in standards.

7. Over the past three months, how have your bank's credit standards for approving applications for CRE loans changed?

	All Respondents		Large Banks		Other Banks	
	Banks	Percent	Banks	Percent	Banks	Percent
Tightened considerably	0	0.0	0	0.0	0	0.0
Tightened somewhat	2	2.7	0	0.0	2	5.7
Remained basically unchanged	55	75.3	30	78.9	25	71.4
Eased somewhat	16	21.9	8	21.1	8	22.9
Eased considerably	0	0.0	0	0.0	0	0.0
Total	73	100.0	38	100.0	35	100.0

8. Apart from normal seasonal variation, how has demand for CRE loans changed over the past three months?

	All Respondents		Large Banks		Other Banks	
	Banks	Percent	Banks	Percent	Banks	Percent
Substantially stronger	2	2.7	1	2.6	1	2.9
Moderately stronger	34	46.6	18	47.4	16	45.7
About the same	36	49.3	18	47.4	18	51.4
Moderately weaker	1	1.4	1	2.6	0	0.0
Substantially weaker	0	0.0	0	0.0	0	0.0
Total	73	100.0	38	100.0	35	100.0

Questions 9-14 ask about changes in standards and demand over the past twelve months for three different types of CRE loans at your bank: construction and land development loans, loans secured by nonfarm nonresidential properties, and loans secured by multifamily residential properties. If your bank's lending policies have not changed over the past twelve months, please report as unchanged even if the policies are restrictive or accommodative relative to longer-term norms. If your bank's policies have tightened or eased over the past twelve months, please so report them regardless of how they stand relative to longer-term norms. Also, please report changes in enforcement of existing policies as changes in policies.

9. Over the past twelve months, how have your bank's credit standards for approving applications for construction and land development loans or credit lines changed?

	All Respondents		Large Banks		Other Banks	
	Banks	Percent	Banks	Percent	Banks	Percent
Tightened considerably	0	0.0	0	0.0	0	0.0
Tightened somewhat	4	5.6	1	2.7	3	8.6
Remained basically unchanged	55	76.4	26	70.3	29	82.9
Eased somewhat	13	18.1	10	27.0	3	8.6
Eased considerably	0	0.0	0	0.0	0	0.0
Total	72	100.0	37	100.0	35	100.0

10. Over the past twelve months, how have your bank's credit standards for approving new applications for loans secured by nonfarm nonresidential properties changed?

	All Respondents		Large Banks		Other Banks	
	Banks	Percent	Banks	Percent	Banks	Percent
Tightened considerably	0	0.0	0	0.0	0	0.0
Tightened somewhat	1	1.4	0	0.0	1	2.9
Remained basically unchanged	53	72.6	25	65.8	28	80.0
Eased somewhat	19	26.0	13	34.2	6	17.1
Eased considerably	0	0.0	0	0.0	0	0.0
Total	73	100.0	38	100.0	35	100.0

11. Over the past twelve months, how have your bank's credit standards for approving new applications for loans secured by multifamily residential properties changed?

	All Respondents		Large Banks		Other Banks	
	Banks	Percent	Banks	Percent	Banks	Percent
Tightened considerably	1	1.4	0	0.0	1	2.9
Tightened somewhat	2	2.8	1	2.7	1	2.9
Remained basically unchanged	42	58.3	15	40.5	27	77.1
Eased somewhat	27	37.5	21	56.8	6	17.1
Eased considerably	0	0.0	0	0.0	0	0.0
Total	72	100.0	37	100.0	35	100.0

12. How has demand for construction and land development loans changed over the past twelve months? (Please consider the number of requests for new spot loans, for disbursement of funds under existing loan commitments, and for new or increased credit lines.)

	All Respondents		Large Banks		Other Banks	
	Banks	Percent	Banks	Percent	Banks	Percent
Substantially stronger	1	1.4	1	2.7	0	0.0
Moderately stronger	35	48.6	17	45.9	18	51.4
About the same	30	41.7	15	40.5	15	42.9
Moderately weaker	5	6.9	3	8.1	2	5.7
Substantially weaker	1	1.4	1	2.7	0	0.0
Total	72	100.0	37	100.0	35	100.0

13. How has demand for loans secured by nonfarm nonresidential properties changed over the past twelve months?

	All Respondents		Large Banks		Other Banks	
	Banks	Percent	Banks	Percent	Banks	Percent
Substantially stronger	0	0.0	0	0.0	0	0.0
Moderately stronger	31	42.5	15	39.5	16	45.7
About the same	40	54.8	21	55.3	19	54.3
Moderately weaker	2	2.7	2	5.3	0	0.0
Substantially weaker	0	0.0	0	0.0	0	0.0
Total	73	100.0	38	100.0	35	100.0

14. How has demand for loans secured by multifamily residential properties changed over the past twelve months?

	All Respondents		Large Banks		Other Banks	
	Banks	Percent	Banks	Percent	Banks	Percent
Substantially stronger	7	9.7	4	10.8	3	8.6
Moderately stronger	33	45.8	17	45.9	16	45.7
About the same	30	41.7	15	40.5	15	42.9
Moderately weaker	2	2.8	1	2.7	1	2.9
Substantially weaker	0	0.0	0	0.0	0	0.0
Total	72	100.0	37	100.0	35	100.0

Questions 15-16 ask about three categories of **residential mortgage loans** at your bank—prime residential mortgages, nontraditional residential mortgages, and subprime residential mortgages. Question 15 deals with changes in your bank's credit standards for loans in each of these categories over the past three months. Question 16 deals with changes in demand for loans in each of these categories over the same period. If your bank's credit standards have not changed over the relevant period, please report them as unchanged even if the standards are either restrictive or accommodative relative to longer-term norms. If your bank's credit standards have tightened or eased over the relevant period, please so report them regardless of how they stand relative to longer-term norms. Also, please report changes in enforcement of existing standards as changes in standards.

For the purposes of this survey, please use the following definitions of these loan categories (note that the loan categories are not mutually exclusive) and include first-lien loans only:

- The **prime** *category of residential mortgages includes loans made to borrowers that typically had relatively strong, well-documented credit histories, relatively high credit scores, and relatively low debt-to-income ratios at the time of origination. This would include fully amortizing loans that have a fixed rate, a standard adjustable rate, or a common hybrid adjustable rate—those for which the interest rate is initially fixed for a multi-year period and subsequently adjusts more frequently.*

- The **nontraditional** *category of residential mortgages includes, but is not limited to, adjustable-rate mortgages with multiple payment options, interest-only mortgages, and ``Alt-A'' products such as mortgages with limited income verification and mortgages secured by non-owner-occupied properties. (Please exclude standard adjustable-rate mortgages and common hybrid adjustable-rate mortgages.)*

- The **subprime** *category of residential mortgages typically includes loans made to borrowers that displayed one or more of the following characteristics at the time of origination: weakened credit histories that include payment delinquencies, chargeoffs, judgments, and/or bankruptcies; reduced repayment capacity as measured by credit scores or debt-to-income ratios; or incomplete credit histories.*

15. Over the past three months, how have your bank's credit standards for approving applications from individuals for mortgage loans to purchase homes changed?

A. Credit standards on mortgage loans that your bank categorizes as prime residential mortgages have:

	All Respondents		Large Banks		Other Banks	
	Banks	Percent	Banks	Percent	Banks	Percent
Tightened considerably	0	0.0	0	0.0	0	0.0
Tightened somewhat	2	3.0	2	5.9	0	0.0
Remained basically unchanged	58	86.6	28	82.4	30	90.9
Eased somewhat	7	10.4	4	11.8	3	9.1
Eased considerably	0	0.0	0	0.0	0	0.0
Total	67	100.0	34	100.0	33	100.0

For this question, 2 respondents answered "My bank does not originate prime residential mortgages."

B. Credit standards on mortgage loans that your bank categorizes as nontraditional residential mortgages have:

	All Respondents		Large Banks		Other Banks	
	Banks	Percent	Banks	Percent	Banks	Percent
Tightened considerably	0	0.0	0	0.0	0	0.0
Tightened somewhat	1	3.1	1	5.6	0	0.0
Remained basically unchanged	28	87.5	15	83.3	13	92.9
Eased somewhat	3	9.4	2	11.1	1	7.1
Eased considerably	0	0.0	0	0.0	0	0.0
Total	32	100.0	18	100.0	14	100.0

For this question, 37 respondents answered "My bank does not originate nontraditional residential mortgages."

C. Credit standards on mortgage loans that your bank categorizes as subprime residential mortgages have:

	All Respondents		Large Banks		Other Banks	
	Banks	Percent	Banks	Percent	Banks	Percent
Tightened considerably	1	25.0	0	0.0	1	33.3
Tightened somewhat	0	0.0	0	0.0	0	0.0
Remained basically unchanged	3	75.0	1	100.0	2	66.7
Eased somewhat	0	0.0	0	0.0	0	0.0
Eased considerably	0	0.0	0	0.0	0	0.0
Total	4	100.0	1	100.0	3	100.0

For this question, 65 respondents answered "My bank does not originate subprime residential mortgages."

16. Apart from normal seasonal variation, how has demand for mortgages to purchase homes changed over the past three months? (Please consider only new originations as opposed to the refinancing of existing mortgages.)

A. Demand for mortgages that your bank categorizes as prime residential mortgages was:

	All Respondents		Large Banks		Other Banks	
	Banks	Percent	Banks	Percent	Banks	Percent
Substantially stronger	1	1.5	1	2.9	0	0.0
Moderately stronger	38	56.7	19	55.9	19	57.6
About the same	22	32.8	12	35.3	10	30.3
Moderately weaker	5	7.5	2	5.9	3	9.1
Substantially weaker	1	1.5	0	0.0	1	3.0
Total	67	100.0	34	100.0	33	100.0

For this question, 2 respondents answered "My bank does not originate prime residential mortgages."

B. Demand for mortgages that your bank categorizes as nontraditional residential mortgages was:

	All Respondents		Large Banks		Other Banks	
	Banks	Percent	Banks	Percent	Banks	Percent
Substantially stronger	0	0.0	0	0.0	0	0.0
Moderately stronger	6	18.8	3	16.7	3	21.4
About the same	21	65.6	11	61.1	10	71.4
Moderately weaker	3	9.4	2	11.1	1	7.1
Substantially weaker	2	6.3	2	11.1	0	0.0
Total	32	100.0	18	100.0	14	100.0

For this question, 37 respondents answered "My bank does not originate nontraditional residential mortgages."

C. Demand for mortgages that your bank categorizes as subprime residential mortgages was:

	All Respondents		Large Banks		Other Banks	
	Banks	Percent	Banks	Percent	Banks	Percent
Substantially stronger	0	0.0	0	0.0	0	0.0
Moderately stronger	1	25.0	0	0.0	1	33.3
About the same	3	75.0	1	100.0	2	66.7
Moderately weaker	0	0.0	0	0.0	0	0.0
Substantially weaker	0	0.0	0	0.0	0	0.0
Total	4	100.0	1	100.0	3	100.0

For this question, 65 respondents answered "My bank does not originate subprime residential mortgages."

*Questions 17-18 ask about **revolving home equity lines of credit** at your bank. Question 17 deals with changes in your bank's credit standards over the past three months. Question 18 deals with changes in demand. If your bank's credit standards have not changed over the relevant period, please report them as unchanged even if they are either restrictive or accommodative relative to longer-term norms. If your bank's credit standards have tightened or eased over the relevant period, please so report them regardless of how they stand relative to longer-term norms. Also, please report changes in enforcement of existing standards as changes in standards.*

17. Over the past three months, how have your bank's credit standards for approving applications for revolving home equity lines of credit changed?

	All Respondents		Large Banks		Other Banks	
	Banks	Percent	Banks	Percent	Banks	Percent
Tightened considerably	0	0.0	0	0.0	0	0.0
Tightened somewhat	2	2.9	1	2.9	1	3.0
Remained basically unchanged	63	92.6	32	91.4	31	93.9
Eased somewhat	3	4.4	2	5.7	1	3.0
Eased considerably	0	0.0	0	0.0	0	0.0
Total	68	100.0	35	100.0	33	100.0

18. Apart from normal seasonal variation, how has demand for revolving home equity lines of credit changed over the past three months? (Please consider only funds actually disbursed as opposed to requests for new or increased lines of credit.)

	All Respondents		Large Banks		Other Banks	
	Banks	Percent	Banks	Percent	Banks	Percent
Substantially stronger	0	0.0	0	0.0	0	0.0
Moderately stronger	17	25.0	9	25.7	8	24.2
About the same	43	63.2	22	62.9	21	63.6
Moderately weaker	8	11.8	4	11.4	4	12.1
Substantially weaker	0	0.0	0	0.0	0	0.0
Total	68	100.0	35	100.0	33	100.0

Questions 19-28 ask about consumer lending at your bank. Question 19 deals with changes in your bank's willingness to make consumer loans over the past three months. Questions 20-25 deal with changes in credit standards and loan terms over the same period. Questions 26-28 deal with changes in demand for consumer loans over the past three months. If your bank's lending policies have not changed over the past three months, please report them as unchanged even if the policies are either restrictive or accommodative relative to longer-term norms. If your bank's policies have tightened or eased over the past three months, please so report them regardless of how they stand relative to longer-term norms. Also, please report changes in enforcement of existing policies as changes in policies.

19. Please indicate your bank's willingness to make consumer installment loans now as opposed to three months ago.

	All Respondents		Large Banks		Other Banks	
	Banks	Percent	Banks	Percent	Banks	Percent
Much more willing	0	0.0	0	0.0	0	0.0
Somewhat more willing	9	13.0	3	8.8	6	17.1
About unchanged	60	87.0	31	91.2	29	82.9
Somewhat less willing	0	0.0	0	0.0	0	0.0
Much less willing	0	0.0	0	0.0	0	0.0
Total	69	100.0	34	100.0	35	100.0

20. Over the past three months, how have your bank's credit standards for approving applications for credit cards from individuals or households changed?

	All Respondents		Large Banks		Other Banks	
	Banks	Percent	Banks	Percent	Banks	Percent
Tightened considerably	0	0.0	0	0.0	0	0.0
Tightened somewhat	1	1.8	0	0.0	1	4.0
Remained basically unchanged	51	92.7	29	96.7	22	88.0
Eased somewhat	3	5.5	1	3.3	2	8.0
Eased considerably	0	0.0	0	0.0	0	0.0
Total	55	100.0	30	100.0	25	100.0

21. Over the past three months, how have your bank's credit standards for approving applications for auto loans to individuals or households changed? (Please include loans arising from retail sales of passenger cars and other vehicles such as minivans, vans, sport-utility vehicles, pickup trucks, and similar light trucks for personal use, whether new or used. Please exclude loans to finance fleet sales, personal cash loans secured by automobiles already paid for, loans to finance the purchase of commercial vehicles and farm equipment, and lease financing.)

	All Respondents		Large Banks		Other Banks	
	Banks	Percent	Banks	Percent	Banks	Percent
Tightened considerably	0	0.0	0	0.0	0	0.0
Tightened somewhat	1	1.6	1	3.1	0	0.0
Remained basically unchanged	53	82.8	24	75.0	29	90.6
Eased somewhat	10	15.6	7	21.9	3	9.4
Eased considerably	0	0.0	0	0.0	0	0.0
Total	64	100.0	32	100.0	32	100.0

22. Over the past three months, how have your bank's credit standards for approving applications for consumer loans other than credit card and auto loans changed?

	All Respondents		Large Banks		Other Banks	
	Banks	Percent	Banks	Percent	Banks	Percent
Tightened considerably	0	0.0	0	0.0	0	0.0
Tightened somewhat	0	0.0	0	0.0	0	0.0
Remained basically unchanged	67	97.1	34	97.1	33	97.1
Eased somewhat	2	2.9	1	2.9	1	2.9
Eased considerably	0	0.0	0	0.0	0	0.0
Total	69	100.0	35	100.0	34	100.0

23. Over the past three months, how has your bank changed the following terms and conditions on new or existing credit card accounts for individuals or households?

a. Credit limits

	All Respondents		Large Banks		Other Banks	
	Banks	Percent	Banks	Percent	Banks	Percent
Tightened considerably	0	0.0	0	0.0	0	0.0
Tightened somewhat	1	2.0	1	3.4	0	0.0
Remained basically unchanged	40	78.4	20	69.0	20	90.9
Eased somewhat	10	19.6	8	27.6	2	9.1
Eased considerably	0	0.0	0	0.0	0	0.0
Total	51	100.0	29	100.0	22	100.0

b. Spreads of interest rates charged on outstanding balances over your bank's cost of funds (wider spreads=tightened, narrower spreads=eased)

	All Respondents		Large Banks		Other Banks	
	Banks	Percent	Banks	Percent	Banks	Percent
Tightened considerably	0	0.0	0	0.0	0	0.0
Tightened somewhat	0	0.0	0	0.0	0	0.0
Remained basically unchanged	48	94.1	27	93.1	21	95.5
Eased somewhat	2	3.9	1	3.4	1	4.5
Eased considerably	1	2.0	1	3.4	0	0.0
Total	51	100.0	29	100.0	22	100.0

c. Minimum percent of outstanding balances required to be repaid each month

	All Respondents		Large Banks		Other Banks	
	Banks	Percent	Banks	Percent	Banks	Percent
Tightened considerably	0	0.0	0	0.0	0	0.0
Tightened somewhat	1	2.0	0	0.0	1	4.5
Remained basically unchanged	49	96.1	28	96.6	21	95.5
Eased somewhat	0	0.0	0	0.0	0	0.0
Eased considerably	1	2.0	1	3.4	0	0.0
Total	51	100.0	29	100.0	22	100.0

d. Minimum required credit score (increased score=tightened, reduced score=eased)

	All Respondents		Large Banks		Other Banks	
	Banks	Percent	Banks	Percent	Banks	Percent
Tightened considerably	0	0.0	0	0.0	0	0.0
Tightened somewhat	0	0.0	0	0.0	0	0.0
Remained basically unchanged	49	96.1	28	96.6	21	95.5
Eased somewhat	2	3.9	1	3.4	1	4.5
Eased considerably	0	0.0	0	0.0	0	0.0
Total	51	100.0	29	100.0	22	100.0

e. The extent to which loans are granted to some customers that do not meet credit scoring thresholds (increased=eased, decreased=tightened)

	All Respondents		Large Banks		Other Banks	
	Banks	Percent	Banks	Percent	Banks	Percent
Tightened considerably	0	0.0	0	0.0	0	0.0
Tightened somewhat	0	0.0	0	0.0	0	0.0
Remained basically unchanged	50	100.0	28	100.0	22	100.0
Eased somewhat	0	0.0	0	0.0	0	0.0
Eased considerably	0	0.0	0	0.0	0	0.0
Total	50	100.0	28	100.0	22	100.0

24. Over the past three months, how has your bank changed the following terms and conditions on loans to individuals or households to purchase autos?

a. Maximum maturity

	All Respondents		Large Banks		Other Banks	
	Banks	Percent	Banks	Percent	Banks	Percent
Tightened considerably	0	0.0	0	0.0	0	0.0
Tightened somewhat	0	0.0	0	0.0	0	0.0
Remained basically unchanged	51	81.0	24	77.4	27	84.4
Eased somewhat	12	19.0	7	22.6	5	15.6
Eased considerably	0	0.0	0	0.0	0	0.0
Total	63	100.0	31	100.0	32	100.0

b. Spreads of loan rates over your bank's cost of funds (wider spreads=tightened, narrower spreads=eased)

	All Respondents		Large Banks		Other Banks	
	Banks	Percent	Banks	Percent	Banks	Percent
Tightened considerably	1	1.6	1	3.2	0	0.0
Tightened somewhat	5	7.9	4	12.9	1	3.1
Remained basically unchanged	38	60.3	18	58.1	20	62.5
Eased somewhat	18	28.6	7	22.6	11	34.4
Eased considerably	1	1.6	1	3.2	0	0.0
Total	63	100.0	31	100.0	32	100.0

c. Minimum required down payment (higher=tightened, lower=eased)

	All Respondents		Large Banks		Other Banks	
	Banks	Percent	Banks	Percent	Banks	Percent
Tightened considerably	0	0.0	0	0.0	0	0.0
Tightened somewhat	0	0.0	0	0.0	0	0.0
Remained basically unchanged	61	96.8	30	96.8	31	96.9
Eased somewhat	2	3.2	1	3.2	1	3.1
Eased considerably	0	0.0	0	0.0	0	0.0
Total	63	100.0	31	100.0	32	100.0

d. Minimum required credit score (increased score=tightened, reduced score=eased)

	All Respondents		Large Banks		Other Banks	
	Banks	Percent	Banks	Percent	Banks	Percent
Tightened considerably	0	0.0	0	0.0	0	0.0
Tightened somewhat	0	0.0	0	0.0	0	0.0
Remained basically unchanged	59	93.7	29	93.5	30	93.8
Eased somewhat	4	6.3	2	6.5	2	6.3
Eased considerably	0	0.0	0	0.0	0	0.0
Total	63	100.0	31	100.0	32	100.0

e. The extent to which loans are granted to some customers that do not meet credit scoring thresholds (increased=eased, decreased=tightened)

	All Respondents		Large Banks		Other Banks	
	Banks	Percent	Banks	Percent	Banks	Percent
Tightened considerably	0	0.0	0	0.0	0	0.0
Tightened somewhat	0	0.0	0	0.0	0	0.0
Remained basically unchanged	60	96.8	30	100.0	30	93.8
Eased somewhat	2	3.2	0	0.0	2	6.3
Eased considerably	0	0.0	0	0.0	0	0.0
Total	62	100.0	30	100.0	32	100.0

25. Over the past three months, how has your bank changed the following terms and conditions on consumer loans *other than* credit card and auto loans?

a. Maximum maturity

	All Respondents		Large Banks		Other Banks	
	Banks	Percent	Banks	Percent	Banks	Percent
Tightened considerably	0	0.0	0	0.0	0	0.0
Tightened somewhat	0	0.0	0	0.0	0	0.0
Remained basically unchanged	68	100.0	35	100.0	33	100.0
Eased somewhat	0	0.0	0	0.0	0	0.0
Eased considerably	0	0.0	0	0.0	0	0.0
Total	68	100.0	35	100.0	33	100.0

b. Spreads of loan rates over your bank's cost of funds (wider spreads=tightened, narrower spreads=eased)

	All Respondents		Large Banks		Other Banks	
	Banks	Percent	Banks	Percent	Banks	Percent
Tightened considerably	0	0.0	0	0.0	0	0.0
Tightened somewhat	2	2.9	1	2.9	1	3.0
Remained basically unchanged	59	86.8	31	88.6	28	84.8
Eased somewhat	7	10.3	3	8.6	4	12.1
Eased considerably	0	0.0	0	0.0	0	0.0
Total	68	100.0	35	100.0	33	100.0

c. Minimum required down payment (higher=tightened, lower=eased)

	All Respondents		Large Banks		Other Banks	
	Banks	Percent	Banks	Percent	Banks	Percent
Tightened considerably	1	1.5	0	0.0	1	3.0
Tightened somewhat	0	0.0	0	0.0	0	0.0
Remained basically unchanged	67	98.5	35	100.0	32	97.0
Eased somewhat	0	0.0	0	0.0	0	0.0
Eased considerably	0	0.0	0	0.0	0	0.0
Total	68	100.0	35	100.0	33	100.0

d. Minimum required credit score (increased score=tightened, reduced score=eased)

	All Respondents		Large Banks		Other Banks	
	Banks	Percent	Banks	Percent	Banks	Percent
Tightened considerably	0	0.0	0	0.0	0	0.0
Tightened somewhat	0	0.0	0	0.0	0	0.0
Remained basically unchanged	66	97.1	34	97.1	32	97.0
Eased somewhat	2	2.9	1	2.9	1	3.0
Eased considerably	0	0.0	0	0.0	0	0.0
Total	68	100.0	35	100.0	33	100.0

e. The extent to which loans are granted to some customers that do not meet credit scoring thresholds (increased=eased, decreased=tightened)

	All Respondents		Large Banks		Other Banks	
	Banks	Percent	Banks	Percent	Banks	Percent
Tightened considerably	0	0.0	0	0.0	0	0.0
Tightened somewhat	0	0.0	0	0.0	0	0.0
Remained basically unchanged	65	97.0	33	97.1	32	97.0
Eased somewhat	2	3.0	1	2.9	1	3.0
Eased considerably	0	0.0	0	0.0	0	0.0
Total	67	100.0	34	100.0	33	100.0

26. Apart from normal seasonal variation, how has demand from individuals or households for credit card loans changed over the past three months?

	All Respondents		Large Banks		Other Banks	
	Banks	Percent	Banks	Percent	Banks	Percent
Substantially stronger	0	0.0	0	0.0	0	0.0
Moderately stronger	8	15.7	4	14.3	4	17.4
About the same	39	76.5	21	75.0	18	78.3
Moderately weaker	4	7.8	3	10.7	1	4.3
Substantially weaker	0	0.0	0	0.0	0	0.0
Total	51	100.0	28	100.0	23	100.0

27. Apart from normal seasonal variation, how has demand from individuals or households for auto loans changed over the past three months?

	All Respondents		Large Banks		Other Banks	
	Banks	Percent	Banks	Percent	Banks	Percent
Substantially stronger	1	1.6	0	0.0	1	3.1
Moderately stronger	18	28.6	10	32.3	8	25.0
About the same	42	66.7	19	61.3	23	71.9
Moderately weaker	2	3.2	2	6.5	0	0.0
Substantially weaker	0	0.0	0	0.0	0	0.0
Total	63	100.0	31	100.0	32	100.0

28. Apart from normal seasonal variation, how has demand from individuals or households for consumer loans other than credit card and auto loans changed over the past three months?

	All Respondents		Large Banks		Other Banks	
	Banks	Percent	Banks	Percent	Banks	Percent
Substantially stronger	1	1.5	1	2.9	0	0.0
Moderately stronger	13	19.1	4	11.8	9	26.5
About the same	51	75.0	27	79.4	24	70.6
Moderately weaker	3	4.4	2	5.9	1	2.9
Substantially weaker	0	0.0	0	0.0	0	0.0
Total	68	100.0	34	100.0	34	100.0

Question 29 asks you to describe the current level of lending standards at your bank relative to the range of standards that has prevailed between 2005 and the present. For each of the loan categories listed below, please consider the points at which standards at your bank were tightest and easiest during this period.

29. Using the range between the tightest and the easiest that lending standards at your bank have been between 2005 and the present, for each of the loan categories listed below, how would you describe the current level of standards relative to that range?

A. C&I loans:

a. New syndicated or club loans (large loans originated by a group of relationship lenders) to investment-grade firms (or unrated firms of similar creditworthiness)

	All Respondents		Large Banks		Other Banks	
	Banks	Percent	Banks	Percent	Banks	Percent
Near the easiest level that standards have been during this period	1	1.5	0	0.0	1	3.4
Significantly easier than the midpoint of the range that standards have been during this period	4	6.2	2	5.6	2	6.9
Somewhat easier than the midpoint of the range that standards have been during this period	20	30.8	16	44.4	4	13.8
Near the midpoint of the range that standards have been during this period	26	40.0	15	41.7	11	37.9
Somewhat tighter than the midpoint of the range that standards have been during this period	6	9.2	2	5.6	4	13.8
Significantly tighter than the midpoint of the range that standards have been during this period	5	7.7	1	2.8	4	13.8
Near the tightest level that standards have been during this period	3	4.6	0	0.0	3	10.3
Total	65	100.0	36	100.0	29	100.0

b. New syndicated or club loans to below-investment-grade firms (or unrated firms of similar creditworthiness)

	All Respondents		Large Banks		Other Banks	
	Banks	Percent	Banks	Percent	Banks	Percent
Near the easiest level that standards have been during this period	0	0.0	0	0.0	0	0.0
Significantly easier than the midpoint of the range that standards have been during this period	4	6.1	2	5.4	2	6.9
Somewhat easier than the midpoint of the range that standards have been during this period	22	33.3	21	56.8	1	3.4
Near the midpoint of the range that standards have been during this period	21	31.8	10	27.0	11	37.9
Somewhat tighter than the midpoint of the range that standards have been during this period	5	7.6	1	2.7	4	13.8
Significantly tighter than the midpoint of the range that standards have been during this period	7	10.6	3	8.1	4	13.8
Near the tightest level that standards have been during this period	7	10.6	0	0.0	7	24.1
Total	66	100.0	37	100.0	29	100.0

c. Non-syndicated loans to large and middle-market firms (annual sales of $50 million or more)

	All Respondents		Large Banks		Other Banks	
	Banks	Percent	Banks	Percent	Banks	Percent
Near the easiest level that standards have been during this period	0	0.0	0	0.0	0	0.0
Significantly easier than the midpoint of the range that standards have been during this period	6	8.6	4	10.8	2	6.1
Somewhat easier than the midpoint of the range that standards have been during this period	22	31.4	16	43.2	6	18.2
Near the midpoint of the range that standards have been during this period	30	42.9	14	37.8	16	48.5
Somewhat tighter than the midpoint of the range that standards have been during this period	6	8.6	2	5.4	4	12.1
Significantly tighter than the midpoint of the range that standards have been during this period	4	5.7	0	0.0	4	12.1
Near the tightest level that standards have been during this period	2	2.9	1	2.7	1	3.0
Total	70	100.0	37	100.0	33	100.0

d. Non-syndicated loans to small firms (annual sales of less than $50 million)

	All Respondents		Large Banks		Other Banks	
	Banks	Percent	Banks	Percent	Banks	Percent
Near the easiest level that standards have been during this period	0	0.0	0	0.0	0	0.0
Significantly easier than the midpoint of the range that standards have been during this period	3	4.5	1	2.9	2	6.1
Somewhat easier than the midpoint of the range that standards have been during this period	18	26.9	14	41.2	4	12.1
Near the midpoint of the range that standards have been during this period	32	47.8	14	41.2	18	54.5
Somewhat tighter than the midpoint of the range that standards have been during this period	9	13.4	4	11.8	5	15.2
Significantly tighter than the midpoint of the range that standards have been during this period	3	4.5	0	0.0	3	9.1
Near the tightest level that standards have been during this period	2	3.0	1	2.9	1	3.0
Total	67	100.0	34	100.0	33	100.0

B. Loans secured by commercial real estate:

a. For construction and land development purposes

	All Respondents		Large Banks		Other Banks	
	Banks	Percent	Banks	Percent	Banks	Percent
Near the easiest level that standards have been during this period	0	0.0	0	0.0	0	0.0
Significantly easier than the midpoint of the range that standards have been during this period	2	2.8	1	2.7	1	2.9
Somewhat easier than the midpoint of the range that standards have been during this period	7	9.9	5	13.5	2	5.9
Near the midpoint of the range that standards have been during this period	18	25.4	10	27.0	8	23.5
Somewhat tighter than the midpoint of the range that standards have been during this period	20	28.2	10	27.0	10	29.4
Significantly tighter than the midpoint of the range that standards have been during this period	16	22.5	7	18.9	9	26.5
Near the tightest level that standards have been during this period	8	11.3	4	10.8	4	11.8
Total	71	100.0	37	100.0	34	100.0

b. For nonfarm nonresidential purposes

	All Respondents		Large Banks		Other Banks	
	Banks	Percent	Banks	Percent	Banks	Percent
Near the easiest level that standards have been during this period	0	0.0	0	0.0	0	0.0
Significantly easier than the midpoint of the range that standards have been during this period	2	2.8	1	2.7	1	2.9
Somewhat easier than the midpoint of the range that standards have been during this period	8	11.3	5	13.5	3	8.8
Near the midpoint of the range that standards have been during this period	28	39.4	15	40.5	13	38.2
Somewhat tighter than the midpoint of the range that standards have been during this period	22	31.0	12	32.4	10	29.4
Significantly tighter than the midpoint of the range that standards have been during this period	9	12.7	4	10.8	5	14.7
Near the tightest level that standards have been during this period	2	2.8	0	0.0	2	5.9
Total	71	100.0	37	100.0	34	100.0

c. For multifamily purposes

	All Respondents		Large Banks		Other Banks	
	Banks	Percent	Banks	Percent	Banks	Percent
Near the easiest level that standards have been during this period	1	1.4	1	2.8	0	0.0
Significantly easier than the midpoint of the range that standards have been during this period	3	4.3	2	5.6	1	2.9
Somewhat easier than the midpoint of the range that standards have been during this period	15	21.4	8	22.2	7	20.6
Near the midpoint of the range that standards have been during this period	25	35.7	14	38.9	11	32.4
Somewhat tighter than the midpoint of the range that standards have been during this period	16	22.9	9	25.0	7	20.6
Significantly tighter than the midpoint of the range that standards have been during this period	8	11.4	2	5.6	6	17.6
Near the tightest level that standards have been during this period	2	2.9	0	0.0	2	5.9
Total	70	100.0	36	100.0	34	100.0

C. Residential real estate:

a. Closed-end loans that your bank categorizes as prime residential mortgages (as described in questions 15A and 16A) with principal balances less than or equal to the conforming loan limits announced by the FHFA (Please include mortgages in high cost areas with loan balances greater than $417,000 that are within the area-specific conforming loan limits (up to $625,500 for fiscal year 2013) determined under the Housing and Economic Recovery Act of 2008. For more information on conforming loan limits, please see: http://www.fhfa.gov/Default.aspx?Page=185.)

	All Respondents		Large Banks		Other Banks	
	Banks	Percent	Banks	Percent	Banks	Percent
Near the easiest level that standards have been during this period	0	0.0	0	0.0	0	0.0
Significantly easier than the midpoint of the range that standards have been during this period	1	1.5	1	3.0	0	0.0
Somewhat easier than the midpoint of the range that standards have been during this period	5	7.6	2	6.1	3	9.1
Near the midpoint of the range that standards have been during this period	29	43.9	16	48.5	13	39.4
Somewhat tighter than the midpoint of the range that standards have been during this period	15	22.7	8	24.2	7	21.2
Significantly tighter than the midpoint of the range that standards have been during this period	10	15.2	4	12.1	6	18.2
Near the tightest level that standards have been during this period	6	9.1	2	6.1	4	12.1
Total	66	100.0	33	100.0	33	100.0

b. Closed-end loans that qualify for a guarantee from the Federal Housing Administration or the U.S. Department of Veterans Affairs

	All Respondents		Large Banks		Other Banks	
	Banks	Percent	Banks	Percent	Banks	Percent
Near the easiest level that standards have been during this period	0	0.0	0	0.0	0	0.0
Significantly easier than the midpoint of the range that standards have been during this period	0	0.0	0	0.0	0	0.0
Somewhat easier than the midpoint of the range that standards have been during this period	4	7.5	2	7.4	2	7.7
Near the midpoint of the range that standards have been during this period	26	49.1	16	59.3	10	38.5
Somewhat tighter than the midpoint of the range that standards have been during this period	12	22.6	4	14.8	8	30.8
Significantly tighter than the midpoint of the range that standards have been during this period	5	9.4	2	7.4	3	11.5
Near the tightest level that standards have been during this period	6	11.3	3	11.1	3	11.5
Total	53	100.0	27	100.0	26	100.0

c. Closed-end loans that your bank categorizes as prime residential mortgages (as described in questions 15A and 16A) with principal balances greater than the conforming loan limits announced by the FHFA

	All Respondents		Large Banks		Other Banks	
	Banks	Percent	Banks	Percent	Banks	Percent
Near the easiest level that standards have been during this period	0	0.0	0	0.0	0	0.0
Significantly easier than the midpoint of the range that standards have been during this period	1	1.6	1	3.0	0	0.0
Somewhat easier than the midpoint of the range that standards have been during this period	4	6.3	2	6.1	2	6.7
Near the midpoint of the range that standards have been during this period	22	34.9	13	39.4	9	30.0
Somewhat tighter than the midpoint of the range that standards have been during this period	18	28.6	9	27.3	9	30.0
Significantly tighter than the midpoint of the range that standards have been during this period	13	20.6	7	21.2	6	20.0
Near the tightest level that standards have been during this period	5	7.9	1	3.0	4	13.3
Total	63	100.0	33	100.0	30	100.0

d. Closed-end loans that your bank categorizes as nontraditional residential mortgages (as described in questions 15B and 16B)

	All Respondents		Large Banks		Other Banks	
	Banks	Percent	Banks	Percent	Banks	Percent
Near the easiest level that standards have been during this period	0	0.0	0	0.0	0	0.0
Significantly easier than the midpoint of the range that standards have been during this period	0	0.0	0	0.0	0	0.0
Somewhat easier than the midpoint of the range that standards have been during this period	2	6.5	1	5.9	1	7.1
Near the midpoint of the range that standards have been during this period	11	35.5	6	35.3	5	35.7
Somewhat tighter than the midpoint of the range that standards have been during this period	7	22.6	4	23.5	3	21.4
Significantly tighter than the midpoint of the range that standards have been during this period	7	22.6	4	23.5	3	21.4
Near the tightest level that standards have been during this period	4	12.9	2	11.8	2	14.3
Total	31	100.0	17	100.0	14	100.0

e. Closed-end loans that your bank categorizes as subprime residential mortgages (as described in questions 15C and 16C)

Responses are not reported when the number of respondents is 3 or fewer.

f. Revolving home equity lines of credit

	All Respondents		Large Banks		Other Banks	
	Banks	Percent	Banks	Percent	Banks	Percent
Near the easiest level that standards have been during this period	0	0.0	0	0.0	0	0.0
Significantly easier than the midpoint of the range that standards have been during this period	0	0.0	0	0.0	0	0.0
Somewhat easier than the midpoint of the range that standards have been during this period	4	6.2	2	6.3	2	6.1
Near the midpoint of the range that standards have been during this period	32	49.2	12	37.5	20	60.6
Somewhat tighter than the midpoint of the range that standards have been during this period	14	21.5	9	28.1	5	15.2
Significantly tighter than the midpoint of the range that standards have been during this period	11	16.9	6	18.8	5	15.2
Near the tightest level that standards have been during this period	4	6.2	3	9.4	1	3.0
Total	65	100.0	32	100.0	33	100.0

D. Consumer lending:

a. Credit card loans that your bank categorizes as prime credit card loans

	All Respondents		Large Banks		Other Banks	
	Banks	Percent	Banks	Percent	Banks	Percent
Near the easiest level that standards have been during this period	0	0.0	0	0.0	0	0.0
Significantly easier than the midpoint of the range that standards have been during this period	2	4.4	1	4.0	1	5.0
Somewhat easier than the midpoint of the range that standards have been during this period	5	11.1	3	12.0	2	10.0
Near the midpoint of the range that standards have been during this period	25	55.6	14	56.0	11	55.0
Somewhat tighter than the midpoint of the range that standards have been during this period	7	15.6	5	20.0	2	10.0
Significantly tighter than the midpoint of the range that standards have been during this period	4	8.9	2	8.0	2	10.0
Near the tightest level that standards have been during this period	2	4.4	0	0.0	2	10.0
Total	45	100.0	25	100.0	20	100.0

b. Credit card loans that your bank categorizes as subprime credit card loans

	All Respondents		Large Banks		Other Banks	
	Banks	Percent	Banks	Percent	Banks	Percent
Near the easiest level that standards have been during this period	0	0.0	0	0.0	0	0.0
Significantly easier than the midpoint of the range that standards have been during this period	0	0.0	0	0.0	0	0.0
Somewhat easier than the midpoint of the range that standards have been during this period	3	12.5	3	23.1	0	0.0
Near the midpoint of the range that standards have been during this period	10	41.7	5	38.5	5	45.5
Somewhat tighter than the midpoint of the range that standards have been during this period	3	12.5	2	15.4	1	9.1
Significantly tighter than the midpoint of the range that standards have been during this period	2	8.3	1	7.7	1	9.1
Near the tightest level that standards have been during this period	6	25.0	2	15.4	4	36.4
Total	24	100.0	13	100.0	11	100.0

c. Auto loans

	All Respondents		Large Banks		Other Banks	
	Banks	Percent	Banks	Percent	Banks	Percent
Near the easiest level that standards have been during this period	0	0.0	0	0.0	0	0.0
Significantly easier than the midpoint of the range that standards have been during this period	2	3.3	1	3.6	1	3.1
Somewhat easier than the midpoint of the range that standards have been during this period	7	11.7	4	14.3	3	9.4
Near the midpoint of the range that standards have been during this period	36	60.0	16	57.1	20	62.5
Somewhat tighter than the midpoint of the range that standards have been during this period	9	15.0	5	17.9	4	12.5
Significantly tighter than the midpoint of the range that standards have been during this period	5	8.3	2	7.1	3	9.4
Near the tightest level that standards have been during this period	1	1.7	0	0.0	1	3.1
Total	60	100.0	28	100.0	32	100.0

d. Consumer loans other than credit card and auto loans

	All Respondents		Large Banks		Other Banks	
	Banks	Percent	Banks	Percent	Banks	Percent
Near the easiest level that standards have been during this period	0	0.0	0	0.0	0	0.0
Significantly easier than the midpoint of the range that standards have been during this period	1	1.5	0	0.0	1	2.9
Somewhat easier than the midpoint of the range that standards have been during this period	5	7.6	3	9.4	2	5.9
Near the midpoint of the range that standards have been during this period	37	56.1	16	50.0	21	61.8
Somewhat tighter than the midpoint of the range that standards have been during this period	14	21.2	8	25.0	6	17.6
Significantly tighter than the midpoint of the range that standards have been during this period	7	10.6	4	12.5	3	8.8
Near the tightest level that standards have been during this period	2	3.0	1	3.1	1	2.9
Total	66	100.0	32	100.0	34	100.0

1. The sample is selected from among the largest banks in each Federal Reserve District. In the table, large banks are defined as those with total domestic assets of $20 billion or more as of March 31, 2013. The combined assets of the 38 large banks totaled $8.0 trillion, compared to $8.3 trillion for the entire panel of 73 banks, and $ 11.7 trillion for all domestically chartered, federally insured commercial banks.

Table 2

Senior Loan Officer Opinion Survey on Bank Lending Practices
at Selected Branches and Agencies of Foreign Banks in the United States [1]

(Status of policy as of July 2013)

Questions 1-6 *ask about commercial and industrial (C&I) loans at your bank. Questions 1-3 deal with changes in your bank's lending policies over the past three months. Questions 4-5 deal with changes in demand for C&I loans over the past three months. Question 6 asks about changes in prospective demand for C&I loans at your bank, as indicated by the volume of recent inquiries about the availability of new credit lines or increases in existing lines. If your bank's lending policies have not changed over the past three months, please report them as unchanged even if the policies are either restrictive or accommodative relative to longer-term norms. If your bank's policies have tightened or eased over the past three months, please so report them regardless of how they stand relative to longer-term norms. Also, please report changes in enforcement of existing policies as changes in policies.*

1. Over the past three months, how have your bank's credit standards for approving applications for C&I loans or credit lines—other than those to be used to finance mergers and acquisitions—changed?

	All Respondents	
	Banks	Percent
Tightened considerably	0	0.0
Tightened somewhat	0	0.0
Remained basically unchanged	20	90.9
Eased somewhat	2	9.1
Eased considerably	0	0.0
Total	22	100.0

2. For applications for C&I loans or credit lines—other than those to be used to finance mergers and acquisitions—that your bank currently is willing to approve, how have the terms of those loans changed over the past three months?

a. Maximum size of credit lines

	All Respondents	
	Banks	Percent
Tightened considerably	0	0.0
Tightened somewhat	1	4.5
Remained basically unchanged	16	72.7
Eased somewhat	5	22.7
Eased considerably	0	0.0
Total	22	100.0

b. Maximum maturity of loans or credit lines

	All Respondents	
	Banks	Percent
Tightened considerably	0	0.0
Tightened somewhat	0	0.0
Remained basically unchanged	21	95.5
Eased somewhat	1	4.5
Eased considerably	0	0.0
Total	22	100.0

c. Costs of credit lines

	All Respondents	
	Banks	Percent
Tightened considerably	0	0.0
Tightened somewhat	0	0.0
Remained basically unchanged	20	90.9
Eased somewhat	2	9.1
Eased considerably	0	0.0
Total	22	100.0

d. Spreads of loan rates over your bank's cost of funds (wider spreads=tightened, narrower spreads=eased)

	All Respondents	
	Banks	Percent
Tightened considerably	1	4.5
Tightened somewhat	0	0.0
Remained basically unchanged	16	72.7
Eased somewhat	5	22.7
Eased considerably	0	0.0
Total	22	100.0

e. Premiums charged on riskier loans

	All Respondents	
	Banks	Percent
Tightened considerably	0	0.0
Tightened somewhat	0	0.0
Remained basically unchanged	18	81.8
Eased somewhat	4	18.2
Eased considerably	0	0.0
Total	22	100.0

f. Loan covenants

	All Respondents	
	Banks	Percent
Tightened considerably	0	0.0
Tightened somewhat	0	0.0
Remained basically unchanged	19	86.4
Eased somewhat	3	13.6
Eased considerably	0	0.0
Total	22	100.0

g. Collateralization requirements

	All Respondents	
	Banks	Percent
Tightened considerably	0	0.0
Tightened somewhat	0	0.0
Remained basically unchanged	21	95.5
Eased somewhat	1	4.5
Eased considerably	0	0.0
Total	22	100.0

h. Use of interest rate floors (more use=tightened, less use=eased)

	All Respondents	
	Banks	Percent
Tightened considerably	0	0.0
Tightened somewhat	1	4.8
Remained basically unchanged	19	90.5
Eased somewhat	1	4.8
Eased considerably	0	0.0
Total	21	100.0

3. If your bank has tightened or eased its credit standards or its terms for C&I loans or credit lines over the past three months (as described in questions 1 and 2), how important have been the following possible reasons for the change?

A. Possible reasons for tightening credit standards or loan terms:

a. Deterioration in your bank's current or expected capital position

	All Respondents	
	Banks	Percent
Not important	3	100.0
Somewhat important	0	0.0
Very important	0	0.0
Total	3	100.0

b. Less favorable or more uncertain economic outlook

	All Respondents	
	Banks	Percent
Not important	2	66.7
Somewhat important	1	33.3
Very important	0	0.0
Total	3	100.0

c. Worsening of industry-specific problems (please specify industries)

	All Respondents	
	Banks	Percent
Not important	2	66.7
Somewhat important	1	33.3
Very important	0	0.0
Total	3	100.0

d. Less aggressive competition from other banks or nonbank lenders (other financial intermediaries or the capital markets)

	All Respondents	
	Banks	Percent
Not important	0	0.0
Somewhat important	3	100.0
Very important	0	0.0
Total	3	100.0

e. Reduced tolerance for risk

	All Respondents	
	Banks	Percent
Not important	2	66.7
Somewhat important	1	33.3
Very important	0	0.0
Total	3	100.0

f. Decreased liquidity in the secondary market for these loans

	All Respondents	
	Banks	Percent
Not important	1	33.3
Somewhat important	2	66.7
Very important	0	0.0
Total	3	100.0

g. Deterioration in your bank's current or expected liquidity position

	All Respondents	
	Banks	Percent
Not important	2	66.7
Somewhat important	1	33.3
Very important	0	0.0
Total	3	100.0

h. Increased concerns about the potential effects of legislative changes, supervisory actions, or accounting standards

	All Respondents	
	Banks	Percent
Not important	1	33.3
Somewhat important	2	66.7
Very important	0	0.0
Total	3	100.0

B. Possible reasons for easing credit standards or loan terms:

a. Improvement in your bank's current or expected capital position

	All Respondents	
	Banks	Percent
Not important	4	44.4
Somewhat important	5	55.6
Very important	0	0.0
Total	9	100.0

b. More favorable or less uncertain economic outlook

	All Respondents	
	Banks	Percent
Not important	2	22.2
Somewhat important	6	66.7
Very important	1	11.1
Total	9	100.0

c. Improvement in industry-specific problems (please specify industries)

	All Respondents	
	Banks	Percent
Not important	8	88.9
Somewhat important	1	11.1
Very important	0	0.0
Total	9	100.0

d. More aggressive competition from other banks or nonbank lenders (other financial intermediaries or the capital markets)

	All Respondents	
	Banks	Percent
Not important	4	44.4
Somewhat important	1	11.1
Very important	4	44.4
Total	9	100.0

e. Increased tolerance for risk

	All Respondents	
	Banks	Percent
Not important	7	77.8
Somewhat important	2	22.2
Very important	0	0.0
Total	9	100.0

f. Increased liquidity in the secondary market for these loans

	All Respondents	
	Banks	Percent
Not important	6	66.7
Somewhat important	1	11.1
Very important	2	22.2
Total	9	100.0

g. Improvement in your bank's current or expected liquidity position

	All Respondents	
	Banks	Percent
Not important	4	44.4
Somewhat important	5	55.6
Very important	0	0.0
Total	9	100.0

h. Reduced concerns about the potential effects of legislative changes, supervisory actions, or accounting standards

	All Respondents	
	Banks	Percent
Not important	8	88.9
Somewhat important	1	11.1
Very important	0	0.0
Total	9	100.0

4. Apart from normal seasonal variation, how has demand for C&I loans changed over the past three months? (Please consider only funds actually disbursed as opposed to requests for new or increased lines of credit.)

	All Respondents	
	Banks	Percent
Substantially stronger	0	0.0
Moderately stronger	4	18.2
About the same	17	77.3
Moderately weaker	1	4.5
Substantially weaker	0	0.0
Total	22	100.0

5. If demand for C&I loans has strengthened or weakened over the past three months (as described in question 4), how important have been the following possible reasons for the change?

A. If stronger loan demand (answer 1 or 2 to question 4), possible reasons:

a. Customer inventory financing needs increased

	All Respondents	
	Banks	Percent
Not important	4	100.0
Somewhat important	0	0.0
Very important	0	0.0
Total	4	100.0

b. Customer accounts receivable financing needs increased

	All Respondents	
	Banks	Percent
Not important	3	75.0
Somewhat important	1	25.0
Very important	0	0.0
Total	4	100.0

c. Customer investment in plant or equipment increased

	All Respondents	
	Banks	Percent
Not important	1	25.0
Somewhat important	3	75.0
Very important	0	0.0
Total	4	100.0

d. Customer internally generated funds decreased

	All Respondents	
	Banks	Percent
Not important	4	100.0
Somewhat important	0	0.0
Very important	0	0.0
Total	4	100.0

e. Customer merger or acquisition financing needs increased

	All Respondents	
	Banks	Percent
Not important	1	25.0
Somewhat important	3	75.0
Very important	0	0.0
Total	4	100.0

f. Customer borrowing shifted to your bank from other bank or nonbank sources because these other sources became less attractive

	All Respondents	
	Banks	Percent
Not important	4	100.0
Somewhat important	0	0.0
Very important	0	0.0
Total	4	100.0

g. Customers' precautionary demand for cash and liquidity increased

	All Respondents	
	Banks	Percent
Not important	3	75.0
Somewhat important	1	25.0
Very important	0	0.0
Total	4	100.0

h. Customers transitioned from commercial real estate loans to C&I loans

	All Respondents	
	Banks	Percent
Not important	4	100.0
Somewhat important	0	0.0
Very important	0	0.0
Total	4	100.0

B. If weaker loan demand (answer 4 or 5 to question 4), possible reasons:

a. Customer inventory financing needs decreased

	All Respondents	
	Banks	Percent
Not important	1	100.0
Somewhat important	0	0.0
Very important	0	0.0
Total	1	100.0

b. Customer accounts receivable financing needs decreased

	All Respondents	
	Banks	Percent
Not important	1	100.0
Somewhat important	0	0.0
Very important	0	0.0
Total	1	100.0

c. Customer investment in plant or equipment decreased

	All Respondents	
	Banks	Percent
Not important	1	100.0
Somewhat important	0	0.0
Very important	0	0.0
Total	1	100.0

d. Customer internally generated funds increased

	All Respondents	
	Banks	Percent
Not important	1	100.0
Somewhat important	0	0.0
Very important	0	0.0
Total	1	100.0

e. Customer merger or acquisition financing needs decreased

	All Respondents	
	Banks	Percent
Not important	0	0.0
Somewhat important	1	100.0
Very important	0	0.0
Total	1	100.0

f. Customer borrowing shifted from your bank to other bank or nonbank sources because these other sources became more attractive

	All Respondents	
	Banks	Percent
Not important	1	100.0
Somewhat important	0	0.0
Very important	0	0.0
Total	1	100.0

g. Customers' precautionary demand for cash and liquidity decreased

	All Respondents	
	Banks	Percent
Not important	1	100.0
Somewhat important	0	0.0
Very important	0	0.0
Total	1	100.0

h. Customers transitioned from C&I loans to commercial real estate loans

	All Respondents	
	Banks	Percent
Not important	1	100.0
Somewhat important	0	0.0
Very important	0	0.0
Total	1	100.0

6. At your bank, apart from normal seasonal variation, how has the number of inquiries from potential business borrowers regarding the availability and terms of new credit lines or increases in existing lines changed over the past three months? (Please consider only inquiries for additional or increased C&I lines as opposed to the refinancing of existing loans.)

	All Respondents	
	Banks	Percent
The number of inquiries has increased substantially	0	0.0
The number of inquiries has increased moderately	4	18.2
The number of inquiries has stayed about the same	17	77.3
The number of inquiries has decreased moderately	1	4.5
The number of inquiries has decreased substantially	0	0.0
Total	22	100.0

Questions 7-8 ask about commercial real estate (CRE) loans at your bank, including construction and land development loans and loans secured by nonfarm nonresidential real estate. Question 7 deals with changes in your bank's standards over the past three months. Question 8 deals with changes in demand. If your bank's lending standards or terms have not changed over the relevant period, please report them as unchanged even if they are either restrictive or accommodative relative to longer-term norms. If your bank's standards or terms have tightened or eased over the relevant period, please so report them regardless of how they stand relative to longer-term norms. Also, please report changes in enforcement of existing standards as changes in standards.

7. Over the past three months, how have your bank's credit standards for approving applications for CRE loans changed?

	All Respondents	
	Banks	Percent
Tightened considerably	0	0.0
Tightened somewhat	0	0.0
Remained basically unchanged	11	84.6
Eased somewhat	2	15.4
Eased considerably	0	0.0
Total	13	100.0

8. Apart from normal seasonal variation, how has demand for CRE loans changed over the past three months?

	All Respondents	
	Banks	Percent
Substantially stronger	1	7.7
Moderately stronger	4	30.8
About the same	6	46.2
Moderately weaker	2	15.4
Substantially weaker	0	0.0
Total	13	100.0

Questions 9-14 ask about changes in standards and demand over the past twelve months for three different types of CRE loans at your bank: construction and land development loans, loans secured by nonfarm nonresidential properties, and loans secured by multifamily residential properties. If your bank's lending policies have not changed over the past twelve months, please report as unchanged even if the policies are restrictive or accommodative relative to longer-term norms. If your bank's policies have tightened or eased over the past twelve months, please so report them regardless of how they stand relative to longer-term norms. Also, please report changes in enforcement of existing policies as changes in policies.

9. Over the past twelve months, how have your bank's credit standards for approving applications for construction and land development loans or credit lines changed?

	All Respondents	
	Banks	Percent
Tightened considerably	1	9.1
Tightened somewhat	1	9.1
Remained basically unchanged	5	45.5
Eased somewhat	4	36.4
Eased considerably	0	0.0
Total	11	100.0

10. Over the past twelve months, how have your bank's credit standards for approving new applications for loans secured by nonfarm nonresidential properties changed?

	All Respondents	
	Banks	Percent
Tightened considerably	0	0.0
Tightened somewhat	0	0.0
Remained basically unchanged	11	84.6
Eased somewhat	2	15.4
Eased considerably	0	0.0
Total	13	100.0

11. Over the past twelve months, how have your bank's credit standards for approving new applications for loans secured by multifamily residential properties changed?

	All Respondents	
	Banks	Percent
Tightened considerably	0	0.0
Tightened somewhat	0	0.0
Remained basically unchanged	10	83.3
Eased somewhat	2	16.7
Eased considerably	0	0.0
Total	12	100.0

12. How has demand for construction and land development loans changed over the past twelve months? (Please consider the number of requests for new spot loans, for disbursement of funds under existing loan commitments, and for new or increased credit lines.)

	All Respondents	
	Banks	Percent
Substantially stronger	0	0.0
Moderately stronger	3	27.3
About the same	8	72.7
Moderately weaker	0	0.0
Substantially weaker	0	0.0
Total	11	100.0

13. How has demand for loans secured by nonfarm nonresidential properties changed over the past twelve months?

	All Respondents	
	Banks	Percent
Substantially stronger	1	7.7
Moderately stronger	2	15.4
About the same	9	69.2
Moderately weaker	1	7.7
Substantially weaker	0	0.0
Total	13	100.0

14. How has demand for loans secured by multifamily residential properties changed over the past twelve months?

	All Respondents	
	Banks	Percent
Substantially stronger	0	0.0
Moderately stronger	3	25.0
About the same	9	75.0
Moderately weaker	0	0.0
Substantially weaker	0	0.0
Total	12	100.0

Question 15 *asks you to describe the current level of lending standards at your bank relative to the range of standards that has prevailed between 2005 and the present. For each of the loan categories listed below, please consider the points at which standards at your bank were tightest and easiest during this period.*

15. Using the range between the tightest and the easiest that lending standards at your bank have been between 2005 and the present, for each of the loan categories listed below, how would you describe the current level of standards relative to that range?

    A. C&I loans:

        a. New syndicated or club loans (large loans originated by a group of relationship lenders) to investment-grade firms (or unrated firms of similar creditworthiness)

	All Respondents	
	Banks	Percent
Near the easiest level that standards have been during this period	2	9.1
Significantly easier than the midpoint of the range that standards have been during this period	2	9.1
Somewhat easier than the midpoint of the range that standards have been during this period	3	13.6
Near the midpoint of the range that standards have been during this period	12	54.5
Somewhat tighter than the midpoint of the range that standards have been during this period	1	4.5
Significantly tighter than the midpoint of the range that standards have been during this period	2	9.1
Near the tightest level that standards have been during this period	0	0.0
Total	22	100.0

b. New syndicated or club loans to below-investment-grade firms (or unrated firms of similar creditworthiness)

	All Respondents	
	Banks	Percent
Near the easiest level that standards have been during this period	2	9.5
Significantly easier than the midpoint of the range that standards have been during this period	1	4.8
Somewhat easier than the midpoint of the range that standards have been during this period	6	28.6
Near the midpoint of the range that standards have been during this period	9	42.9
Somewhat tighter than the midpoint of the range that standards have been during this period	0	0.0
Significantly tighter than the midpoint of the range that standards have been during this period	2	9.5
Near the tightest level that standards have been during this period	1	4.8
Total	21	100.0

c. Non-syndicated loans to large and middle-market firms (annual sales of $50 million or more)

	All Respondents	
	Banks	Percent
Near the easiest level that standards have been during this period	1	5.6
Significantly easier than the midpoint of the range that standards have been during this period	0	0.0
Somewhat easier than the midpoint of the range that standards have been during this period	7	38.9
Near the midpoint of the range that standards have been during this period	7	38.9
Somewhat tighter than the midpoint of the range that standards have been during this period	1	5.6
Significantly tighter than the midpoint of the range that standards have been during this period	2	11.1
Near the tightest level that standards have been during this period	0	0.0
Total	18	100.0

d. Non-syndicated loans to small firms (annual sales of less than $50 million)

	All Respondents	
	Banks	Percent
Near the easiest level that standards have been during this period	1	9.1
Significantly easier than the midpoint of the range that standards have been during this period	0	0.0
Somewhat easier than the midpoint of the range that standards have been during this period	2	18.2
Near the midpoint of the range that standards have been during this period	3	27.3
Somewhat tighter than the midpoint of the range that standards have been during this period	0	0.0
Significantly tighter than the midpoint of the range that standards have been during this period	3	27.3
Near the tightest level that standards have been during this period	2	18.2
Total	11	100.0

B. Loans secured by commercial real estate:

a. For construction and land development purposes

	All Respondents	
	Banks	Percent
Near the easiest level that standards have been during this period	0	0.0
Significantly easier than the midpoint of the range that standards have been during this period	1	9.1
Somewhat easier than the midpoint of the range that standards have been during this period	2	18.2
Near the midpoint of the range that standards have been during this period	4	36.4
Somewhat tighter than the midpoint of the range that standards have been during this period	0	0.0
Significantly tighter than the midpoint of the range that standards have been during this period	2	18.2
Near the tightest level that standards have been during this period	2	18.2
Total	11	100.0

b. For nonfarm nonresidential purposes

	All Respondents	
	Banks	Percent
Near the easiest level that standards have been during this period	0	0.0
Significantly easier than the midpoint of the range that standards have been during this period	1	7.7
Somewhat easier than the midpoint of the range that standards have been during this period	4	30.8
Near the midpoint of the range that standards have been during this period	5	38.5
Somewhat tighter than the midpoint of the range that standards have been during this period	0	0.0
Significantly tighter than the midpoint of the range that standards have been during this period	1	7.7
Near the tightest level that standards have been during this period	2	15.4
Total	13	100.0

c. For multifamily purposes

	All Respondents	
	Banks	Percent
Near the easiest level that standards have been during this period	0	0.0
Significantly easier than the midpoint of the range that standards have been during this period	2	16.7
Somewhat easier than the midpoint of the range that standards have been during this period	2	16.7
Near the midpoint of the range that standards have been during this period	5	41.7
Somewhat tighter than the midpoint of the range that standards have been during this period	0	0.0
Significantly tighter than the midpoint of the range that standards have been during this period	1	8.3
Near the tightest level that standards have been during this period	2	16.7
Total	12	100.0

1. As of March 31, 2013, the 22 respondents had combined assets of $1.1 trillion, compared to $2.2 trillion for all foreign related banking institutions in the United States. The sample is selected from among the largest foreign-related banking institutions in those Federal Reserve Districts where such institutions are common.